THE THIRD RADFORDS

A PIONEER ADVENTURE

RADFORDS- CANADA

M·S.

JOAN KEY

Martel Publications,
101 - 141 Bushby St.,
Victoria B.C.
V8S 1B3

Canadian Cataloguing in Publication Data

Key, Joan, 1902–
    The third Radfords : a pioneer adventure

    ISBN 0-9692944-1-7

    1. Key, Joan, 1902–   2. Frontier and pioneer life – Prairie Provinces. 3. Prairie Provinces – Biography. 4. Pioneers – Prairie Provinces – Biography. I. Title.
FC3242.K49 1988   971.2'02'0924   C88-091136-0
F1060.9.K49 1988

Printed and bound in Canada by

Hignell Printing Ltd.,

Winnipeg, Manitoba

This book is dedicated to my Mother and Father and to Laetitia.

It is also dedicated to the Colonist Pioneers of the Strathmore and Nightingale Districts.

My thanks to my sisters, relatives and friends who encouraged me to write my recollections of our Prairie days, and my appreciation and thanks to Ursula, Michele, Myrtle and George for their assistance.

CONTENTS

Joan Key in her Victoria Condominium

Introduction

As I write this, from my window I can see far out over the Straits of Juan de Fuca, a helicopter with a load of supplies slung from its undercarriage, beating its way to Trial Island Lighthouse. In the hazy distance the Olympic Mountains hump their blue shoulders against the soft, misty sky, and a drifting log with a row of statuesque, immobile cormorants evenly spaced on it, floats slowly past on the outgoing tide.

As I listen to the faint droning throb of the helicopter, fading into the distance, my mind slips back seventy years or so to the still, autumn days at Radfords, our prairie home. Then the hum of the threshing machines in the fields of grain could be heard from dawn to dusk and, when the weather was threatening, on into the night. Men, women and horses (and sometimes children) worked long hours to get the precious grain stored before the snow fell.

Then as the days darkened and the snowflakes drifted down, we spent long evenings in the warm, lamplit kitchen. Often as Mother read to us, memories of my happy childhood in England would drift through my mind, and I would dream of those carefree days.

Joan Key,
Victoria, British Columbia

My England

"Most of us have certain childish memories
which we can never repeat, since they
represent moments when life was in utter
harmony and sense and spirit perfectly
tuned."
        John Buchan, Memory Hold-the-Door

The year 1909 was a very special year for
me. I was six years old and I think that some
kindly deity deliberately sharpened my senses, my
awareness, of all the wonderful things to be
seen, smelled, felt and heard, during that
magical Spring, Summer and Autumn, and became
memories stored away in my head for the days to
come. If I had grown up in England and such
experiences had been repeated year after year
they would have become ordinary, accepted, and
the wonderment and magic would have faded. As it
seems to me, so much that I experienced during
that lovely mystical year, was permanently
photographed on my mind, and became lifelong
nostalgic memories, because this was to become
our last year in England, and from then on life
would be so different.
    These memories float through my mind like
golden butterflies on the summer breeze. Burying
my face in a tight nosegay of primroses, fresh
picked from under the hedges, and drinking in the
sweet, delicate perfume; with a crooked stick
hauling down the high branches of the blackberry
tangles around Glastonbury Abbey, so that Mother
could gather the luscious dark purple berries;
picking cowslips and kingcups in the green hedge
rimmed meadows; making daisy chains; the gentle
soughing of the wind in the boughs of the trees
far above my head; the mysterious sighing of the
telephone wires. For the first time I heard the
insistent cuckoos calling "Cuck - oo-oo?
Cuck-oo-oo" in the shady woods.
    For the holidays that summer, the family went

to the seaside at Lynmouth in North Devon,(or was it Croyde that year?) and Uncle Dick took me shrimping. With my dress tucked into the waist of my white calico knickers, I paddled about, swishing the net on its long stick through the deep tidal pools, and listening to the slapping of the waves breaking on the beach below, and then the slow sucking sound as the water receded over the pebbles. For a penny-a-ride we went up and down on the "vehicular" to the top of the craggy cliff high above the beach. We were shut into a little iron cage and sat side by side as it was hoisted up the steep cliff, creaking and jerking.

Another memory-picture - seeing Yeovil on a clear, frosty evening, and it must have been the first time I consciously saw the World after dark. I was with somebody, someone was holding my hand as we stood at the top of a rise that looked down over the town, nestled in the valley of the river Yeo. A street or road wound down the incline ahead of us. All daylight had drained away; the world and sky were a deep, dark velvety blue, and I could just see the shapes of houses and buildings below, and the tiny sparks of gas lamps strung along the streets, twinkling in the darkness. Beyond, on the far side of the valley, the faint outline of the rolling hills showed against a streak of translucent sky. It was a mystical experience, and I can shut my eyes and again see that beautiful vision, as clearly as on that long ago evening, and feel my wonderment at the mystery of the night.

No shadows darkened my days. I knew nothing of suffering or sorrow or cruelty, and if there were any family disagreements they were beyond my ken. And then came the spring of 1910 and the great change to the hard, primitive life on the treeless prairie. To me England became more and more a land of fantasy, a land of endless peace and beauty and happiness, a land of great trees that swayed their graceful branches across the filmy blue sky; of smooth green lawns; of

3

Mother's tea parties in the garden, when the
delicious smell of fresh-brewed tea and cucumber
sandwiches mingled with the peculiar aroma of
mowed grass, of children's parties in the
Christmas season, or for birthdays, to which we
were driven in a hansom cab, dressed in frilly
frocks of embroidered India muslin and white lace
mittens, of uncles and aunts and cousins, and
Grandmother, sitting in her special chair in the
drawing-room with her stiff black moire silk
dress swirling out over her little black kid
slippers, and on her head a snow-white pleated
cap with its widow's black velvet bow.

Grandfather Pardon's home -
the first Radfords.

Edith Petter, the author's mother ready to go riding at Yeovil, England.

Harry Petter, the author's father at Radfords, in England.

Departure — Voyage — Interlude

The great surge of emigration was at its peak and the waves of colonists were flooding out from Britain towards the Land of Promise, Canada, the Golden West, and every soul was convinced that within a few short years he would be returning to his homeland a wealthy man.

Harry Petter, his wife Edith and their five children, all girls, aged eighteen and a half months to seven years, were leaving their comfortable home, their many relatives and friends and emigrating to Canada. To Father it was an exciting adventure, the sort of thing he had dreamed of doing all his life. To Mother, it was a rather alarming step into an unkown future, but she was facing it bravely, an obedient Edwardian wife.

"In the Year Nineteen Hundred and Ten -
Where, oh where shall we all be then?"
My Father sang this cheerfully in his fine, clear baritone many times in the autumn of 1909. It was the chorus of a popular song of the time, sung in the music halls and by the pierrots on the piers in summer time. He was busy supervising the packing of all our belongings, even the drawing room furniture, as nobody for a moment doubted we would have another drawingroom in Canada. The cream and pink, glazed-chintz covered chairs and sofa, the rosewood cabinet for Mother's collection of Goss china, the great black piano with the brass candlesticks, Father's mahogany desk, all were being crated and packed ready for our journey to the fabulous, brave New World, where we were to make a wonderful new life for ourselves.

The heavy Jacobean gateleg table, the three carved oak chests, the Glastonbury chairs, and an item that was to prove more valuable to us during the prairie winters than anything else, the iron Nautilus heater, were all carefully packed.

The Nautilus heater was an innovation in England, designed by Grandfather James Petter and made in his foundry in Yeovil. It was shaped like a large nautilus shell, made of heavy iron and set on four legs. The enclosed firebox was built into the lower part of the curve, with two little doors which could be opened when the coal fire was glowing. There was a stovepipe leading back and up into the chimney, creating a good draft. The fluted back and sides flared out like the curved sides of the shell, sending the heat out into the room, the whole thing being a much better source of heat than the traditional open fireplace, where so much of the heat went up the chimney. All this and much more was to be shipped by train to Liverpool, then by steamship to St. John, New Brunswick, on by train to Alberta, and eventually hauled over the prairie trails on wagons and six-horse teams, to our new home.

We left our home, the second Radfords, in Yeovil, Somerset, on March 30th, 1910 on a cold wet and windy morning. Aunts and Uncles, cousins and Grandmother were down at the great drafty, roofed station to see us off. I can still remember the heavy acrid smell of coal smoke that hung in the damp air.

Grandmother had not been greatly impressed with the glowing reports of life in the new world. She had read about the Arctic explorations of Amundsen and Scott, and feared we might find ourselves in that cruel land of icebergs and blizzards. So she had her dressmaker fashion five strange garments for the children. They were like the habits of medieval monks, of heavy wool cloth. Betty's, Barbara's and mine were brown, and the twins were scarlet.They reached to the ground, were belted around the waist, and had hoods, which we could wear on our heads, or hanging down our backs. We were all dressed up in them to start out on the great voyage, and must have been a quaint looking little group. Mother removed them before we reached Liverpool, replacing them with our ordinary coats and hats, and to the best of my memory we never saw them again.

Grandmother Petter, four years widowed, frail and a little stooped, stood quietly among the chattering, excited group on the platform. There was a faraway look in her eyes, and I wonder now if she knew in her heart that she was seeing her eldest son, who had been her comfort and mainstay, for the last time. She died two years later.

Earlier in the year Mother had travelled down to her family home, the first Radfords, at Dawlish in Devonshire, to say goodbye to her father, brothers and sisters.

His blue eyes shining with excitement Father was bustling about, his hands full of tickets and folders, organizing the pile of valises, portmanteaux, boxes and a large leather-strapped wicker hamper, and supervising the loading of it all into the goods van. He was thirty-nine years old, and had cheerfuflly sold his share in the family foundry to his brothers, so that he could now realize his great ambition of emigrating to a new country, and hopefully making a fortune. His tweed cloth cap sat jauntily on top of his thick, curly hair, which Mother boasted had once been the colour of a sovereign, but which was now already turning to silver.

On the windy station platform, Mother was holding one of the twins in her arms, and Mary Ann Bottomley, Mother's right hand and standby, who was going to Canada with us, held the other. Laetitia and Sissie were not yet two years old, and of course were rather confused and alarmed by all the commotion. Barbara, (who had been nicknamed "Tommy" by Father who had been so disappointed when the third baby had turned out to be another girl),Betty and I, were being made a great fuss of by the Aunts and Uncles, and were racing about among the grownups, shouting and laughing, and tripping over our long habits.

The train was puffing and panting, the baggage was all loaded, and we were soon climbing aboard. The last goodbyes were shouted from the carriage windows, the thin, shrill whistle knifed through the chilly air, and then the wheels began to grind. We were off on our way to the Promised Land.

Later that day we reached Liverpool, and that same evening we boarded the steamship Lake Manitoba. It was a small ship, crowded with colonists, and as the crossing from the first day was particularly rough, almost everybody on board was seasick. The ship rolled like a barrel. The heady atmosphere of adventure and excitement that had pervaded the ship with the colonists, faded rapidly, and the women passengers and most of the men and children took to their cabins. Mother and Mary Ann, who we called "Boppo", along with the twins, took to their berths, and Father who was a good sailor, had to look after the rest of us. I was fortunately not seasick, and left to myself managed to explore the ship from steerage to fo'c'sle, and undoubtedly made a thorough nuisance of myself. I was a clumsy, absent-minded child, always, and probably intentionally, forgetting what I was told. I remember running down one of the red-carpeted corridors with an exasperated stewardess running after me. I had stepped in some tarry mess, and was leaving black sticky footsteps wherever I went.

Before leaving home Aunt Eva had given me a particularly lovely doll, a china doll with real hair and blue eyes that opened and shut. She had dressed it beautifully as a bride, every stitch done by hand. Helen had a long, full cream coloured satin dress with a train, a floating lace veil with a wreath of orange blossoms, and tiny white kid slippers. This day I had been standing in the stern of the ship, leaning precariously over the rail, watching the wind whipped, boiling wake, with the doll in my arms. Unfortunately, the strong gale whistling across my head, almost whisked my blue sailor cap off, and in clutching it, I dropped Helen overboard. It should have been a sad loss, but for some reason it seemed to me an exciting adventure, and dramatic experience. Another child my age would have probably shrieked in dismay and rushed to her mother with tears streaming down her cheeks,but it had not affected me in that way at all.

Fascinated, I watched her bobbing up and down on the crest of the curling waves, her white satin dress billowing out and holding her up for a few moments, and then she twirled slowly and sank out of sight. I stared at the green foam-laced waves and wondered what it would feel like to float down into all that bubbly water. Was Helen now in a lovely liquid world of mermaids and floating seaweed? Would it be like little Tom, the chimney sweep in Charles Kingsley's "The Water Babies", with a kindly Mrs. Do-As-You-Would-Be-Done-By looking after her?

The thought of death and drowning, or the realization that I had lost forever a beautiful creation, which might eventually become a treasured family heirloom didn't for a moment enter my head. To me my doll was now a fairy story heroine, and for a moment I almost envied her. I told nobody about this experience, and with all that was to happen in the days to come, she was missed by no one but myself.

We landed at St. John, New Brunswick and after spending a long depressing day in a huge immigration shed, surrounded by hundreds of other bewildered and somewhat worried colonists, and mountains of baggage of all descriptions, as we went through the customs and immigration procedures, we finally got ourselves on a train for Montreal. I don't remember much about the long trip, but Uncle Claude, Father's younger brother, who had emigrated to America a few years earlier, and was now in the glove-making business in New York State, came up to Montreal to see us. He boarded our train, and continued on with us for a few hours before catching another train back to Montreal and then on down to Gloversville, New York. He brought us all extravagant presents, and was very jolly and encouraging, promising to visit us when we were settled. He never did. He shortly after met and married an American girl, Janet Zimmerman, and was too busy making a living and raising his family to travel all the way to Alberta.

There was one episode on the journey through the then almost uninhabited forests of Northern Ontario which I well remember. Some abandoned freight cars blocked the line and our train was held up for several hours. The passengers disembarked and we explored the strange deep woods, craggy, mossy rocks and streams.

Eventually we arrived in Winnipeg, the grown-ups discouraged and exhausted, the children excited and unruly, from being cooped up in the stuffy carriages. Father took a couple of rooms in a small hotel near the station, and we were to board a train that evening for Grandview, some hundred and fifty miles north-west of Winnipeg. There we were to stay with Father's cousin, May Holman, and her husband and four children, on their homestead, while Father went on to Alberta to take up the half section the C.P.R. was holding for him, and to build a house for us.

It was very hot that April day in Winnipeg, and by late afternoon alarming black storm clouds were boiling up in the north west. Brilliant flashes of lightning flared out from the storm centre, followed by great claps of thunder. Then the wind and hail lashed over the city; the vicious lightning, green, blue and orange, seemed to flash incessantly from all directions and the thunder crashed and roared over us. The storm terrified Mother, she declared that Canada was no place for us, and Father should make arrangements to return to England immediately. We had never experienced such wild and fearful weather there! Father thought the storm rather exciting, and said that of course there could be no turning back now. As the storm gradually lessened its fury, passing on to the east, the temperature dropped rapidly, and in half an hour freezing rain and sleet were falling. By the time we were to board the train it was bitterly cold.

The trip in a primitive, cold and uncomfortable carriage, on a side line running north to Dauphin and Grandview, must have been a terrible and bewildering experience for our parents. Leaving in the evening, we travelled through the night, the passengers sitting up on the hard seats, the children wrapped up in coats and blankets, and made as comfortable as possible. The train jolted and swayed, stopping at many mysterious little stations, where two or three muffled figures swinging dim hurricane lanterns hurried about in the darkness. Then the train would pull away and the dim huddle of little buildings would fade into the swirling snowflakes like dreams in the night. The rain and sleet had turned to snow and the train seemed to crawl through the blizzard into the unknown.

We arrived in Grandview about five in the morning, just as the first faint streak of grey light of pre-dawn was showing on the horizon. The storm was over, and the snow already turning to slush, but it was cold as we stood, sleepy and bewildered, on the planks of the station platform. We could see a few shadowy buildings scattered about, but there was not a light in any of these.

Uncle Will Holman was to be there to meet us but the storm had delayed him and he had not yet arrived. The train stood for a while, with the huge engine sending forth blasts of hissing white steam into the chill air, and the powerful beam of the headlight shooting down the track into the dark. Then with clanging bell and much puffing and squealing it pulled away and we were left behind in the bleak, still night.

At last with thankfulness we heard the creaking of wagon wheels, and a team and wagon pulled up to the wooden platform. Uncle Will climbed down and shook Father's hand, and then an elderly man, small and wizened, who turned out to be his farm hand, followed with a democrat. We were packed into the two vehicles, with all our

baggage, and driven some miles, jolting and
swaying over the rutted, muddy road, to the
Holman homestead. Despite having four young
children of their own, Aunt May and Uncle Will,
with true western hospitality, took the eight
weary, confused, and disillusioned travellers,
into their small farm home and made us welcome.

William Holman had emigrated to America from
England in 1890 and five years later had taken up
a homestead of 160 acres, near Grandview, in
Manitoba, for which he paid $10.00 - to cover the
paper work! His wife, May Page, our Father's
first cousin, joined him later, and their four
children were born on the farm. "Uncle Will" as
we called him, was a gentle, quiet man, with
thick reddish-brown hair and blue eyes. "Aunt
May", her dark brown hair swept smoothly back
from her face and swirled up at the back, quietly
coped with all the problems of caring for and
feeding her family and the eight visitors in that
farm kitchen, primitive as were all farm kitchens
at that time. Covered with a print overall apron,
buttoned down her back, she cooked the huge meals
three times a day on a wood fired cookstove,
baked bread and pies, and must have worked from
dawn to dark. No doubt Mother and Mary Ann,
"Boppo" as we nicknamed her, stood by, perhaps
peeling potatoes, stoking the stove, and washing
the mountains of dishes, but would not have been
much help otherwise.

Father, after a couple days rest continued on
to Alberta, but the rest of us stayed on with our
cousins for about two months. Boppo and we five
girls slept in a large attic room, on home made
wooden beds, and we used this for a playroom on
wet days, inventing all kinds of noisy games.

I have wonderful memories of the hilarious
times we six older children had, as we explored
the scrubby poplar bluffs, the creeks and ponds,
that covered the countryside around the Holman
farm, so different to the smooth green fields,
hedges and flower filled woods of Somerset.

Irene, called Millie, eight years old,

Edith, a year younger, and Alfred, five, teased us unmercifully, making fun of our English accents, and our queer, inappropriate clothes. Our innocent minds made us fair game, as they told us fantastic stories of prairie wolves devouring little children, Indians in warpaint and feathers who might kidnap us, of huge packrats, porcupines that would shoot quills at us, and even grizzlybears. To be fair to them, it was all done in fun and we were fascinated, not sure how much we could believe, but we longed to see prairie wolves, packrats and grizzly bears.

Millie, Edie and Alfred went to the local public school, leaving early in the morning to walk the two miles, carrying lunches in lard pails. We envied them, especially when they told impressive stories at the supper table of their academic achievements, and their prowess at baseball during recess. As we had never been to school it all sounded very exciting, much more so than the "lessons" we had had, five mornings a week from Aunt Eva, in the dining room at Grandmother's home in Yeovil.

One day when Tommy and I were running down a cart track that wound through a dense bit of bluff, we came face to face with a strange animal. He was beautiful in his spring finery of sparkling white and shiny black, and stood calmly facing us wwith a benevolent look on his little pointed face. We crept towards him, holding out our hands, he seemed friendly and tame and we thought it would be fun to pat him. Suddenly there was a scream, and we saw Millie standing some distance down the path behind the animal. She must have seen us, and realized what we were planning to do. "Run! Run! That's a skunk, go back, or he will squirt you!" Terrified, our hair standing on end, we raced back towards the farm, not quite sure what horror was after us. Some time later we realized what we had escaped, when Shep, the Holman collie dog, a beautiful beast with a long, thick, golden and white coat, had an encounter with a skunk. He smelled so horrible for weeks afterwards, in spite of being scrubbed with soapsuds in the creek, that nobody would go near him. He was obviously humiliated, and slunk about the farmyard looking miserable.

While we were staying with our cousins, during which time we were having such an exciting and happy time, I had an experience which sobered me for the moment, and gave me something to ponder in time to come.

One sunny morning Mother took Betty and me by the hand, and one on each side of her we walked out into the marshy, sweet smelling bush below the farmhouse. It was springtime, the trees were bursting into leaf, the sun was warm and the busy chirping birds were flying about in the branches. We came to a mossy little glen where the sunlight shimmered through the quivering aspen leaves. Mother sat down on a stump, and we explored a little stream, creek, we learned to call it. Sometime later I went back to Mother who was still sitting on the stump. To my dismay, she sat with her face in her hands, her eyes closed, and tears were running down her face. I stood in front of her, staring at her until she noticed me, then she took her hanky out of her pocket, mopped her face, and smiled at me.

"It's all right, dear, nothing to worry about. I am just a little bit homesick".

No doubt this was one of the steps that children have to take in the growing up process, a jolt that brings an awareness to us that life for grown people is not all happiness, smooth and carefree, that men and women, as well as children, weep.

Some special memories of that time were the taste of the delicious jelly Aunt May made from the wild high-bush cranberries that grew in Northern Manitoba, and the fragrant smell of the smoke of last year's stubble being burned off the fields in preparation for the spring ploughing. With much excitement we watched Uncle Will and his farm hand walking up and down the fire line, wielding hayforks to keep it under control.

Behind the house, outside the kitchen door was a great pile of split logs, firewood for the cookstove, aromatic poplar, drying in the sunshine, and it had a very special perfume.

At last, about the middle of June, a letter came from father telling us that the house was almost ready and that we could start on our way. Valises and portmanteaux were packed once more and Aunt May filled generous baskets of food for the journey. We said goodbye to the cousins, and it must have been with a feeling of relief that they looked forward to settling down again to their normal existence.

We piled into the wagon once more, and Uncle Will drove us into town where we boarded the train to Winnipeg. The train left Grandview about midnight and so once more we travelled through the night. In Winnipeg we had to transfer ourselves and all our baggage from the C.N.R. station to the C.P.R. station, and this time we did not have Father to organize all the arrangements. Eventually Mother and the faithful Boppo, exhausted as they must have been, got us safely aboard the already crowded colonist train, and we were on our way to Alberta.

Father's Memories

After a couple of days of relaxation with the Holman family, during which Uncle Will and Father had long talks, and kindly Uncle Will gave Father much good advice on selecting farmland, the best breeds of cattle and horses to choose, and the farm implements he would need, Father, his confidence and enthusiasm renewed continued on his journey to Strathmore. Uncle Will drove him into Grandview in his buggy to catch the train, and Betty and I went with them. Father stood on the steps of the train as it pulled out of the station, small leather bag in one hand, and waved his hat to us as the train gathered speed. The following weeks must have been a traumatic experience for him.

Many years later in the summer of 1942 Father was very ill. We knew his condition was serious, and his five daughters came to visit him from time to time. During these visits, as I sat by his bedside, he dictated to me his memories of the Strathmore days. He lay there against the pillows, recalling the adventures, excitement and challenges of those times, and his blue eyes would momentarily sparkle as he chuckled at some particular memory.

"Soon after arriving at Strathmore I found myself sharing a room with another man. The one little hotel, the King Edward, was full to overflowing with the newcomers and accommodation of any kind was hard to find. My room-mate turned out to be a real estate man, and he advised me to return to Brooks some forty five miles east of Strathmore, as there was fine farmland in that area, before deciding on the C.P.R. acreage at Nightingale. So the next day I took the train to Brooks, and found it booming, natural gas having just been discovered in that area. The town was packed with excited speculators, promoters and opportunists of all kinds.

On enquiring about a hotel I was told there

was none, but was referred to a rooming house. There I was told it was full, but I was offered a cot in an attic to be shared with six other men. I did not relish this, and I decided to acquire a sleeping bag, and walk out on the open prairie and sleep under the stars. The weather was sunny and warm during the day, but I knew it would be very cold at night. On my way out of town I passed a carpenter who was building a house, and knowing I would soon have to build one myself, I thought I might pick up some helpful advice. The kindly carpenter helped me with many suggestions, and then asked me where I was going. When I told him I was going to sleep out on the prairie he said, "You had better come with me. I sleep in quite a good place." Though I was disappointed at missing my adventurous night under the stars, I felt I could not refuse so kind an offer. We then went to the butcher shop, where the carpenter explained he slept with two very decent men. To my amazement, I found we were to sleep in the shop itself, where meat was lying about on the counters, and hanging from the walls and ceiling, some of it smelling none too fresh. Looking around, I thought the shop window might be the best place to spread my sleeping bag, even if I would be in full view of the street. Instead of glass, the window was covered with mosquito netting, and so the air was fresher. I crawled into the sleeping bag, and dead tired soon dropped off to sleep. About 2 A.M. we were awakened, as six noisy, dirty drunks pushed their way into the shop shouting and quarrelling, and still worse, spitting and hawking. They settled down on the floor after a while and I managed to catch a little more sleep. I decided that I would on no account eat meat while in Brooks.

The next morning I joined a large party to be driven in democrats to inspect the land recommended by the real estate salesman. It was a very dry year, no rain had fallen for nine months and the snowfall had been unusually light the preceding winter. The prairie grass was already brown and brittle, the sloughs almost dry, with green slime spreading over what little water was left. We had very little water to drink, and for two days the poor horses were without any. We had no water for washing or shaving, and on returning to Strathmore by train, after visiting Brooks, I, who had been rather shocked by the unshaven and grubby appearance of most of the men I had met, (although many seemed to be well educated under their rough exteriors), was walking down the corridor of the train and found myself approaching an even tougher looking individual than any I had yet seen. I was shocked to find I was facing a mirror on the car door at the end of the passage, and that the terrible looking apparition was myself! I then realized that I had been unable to wash or shave for several days. My men friends told me that I had absorbed the ways of the country very rapidly.

The following day I hired a buggy and horse from the livery stable and drove out to inspect the half section the C.P.R. was holding for me. This was eight miles north of Strathmore and about two miles south of Nightingale. I knew very little about land, soil, or how to judge the potential of the property as a prospect for successful farming, but I saw some charming wild flowers, birds were singing in the wild rose bushes, and towards the east I could see the gleam of water on a small lake. I thought it all looked much more attractive than the flat, dry country we had seen around Brooks, and I decided I would settle for it.

Will Holman sent a carpenter, who had worked for him, out from Grandview, to help me build our house. Mr. Lane arrived and the building of the house proceeded. It was intended to build a design prepared by my brother John, an architect, before we left England, but this was found to be quite unsuitable for this climate. A plan from a book provided by the lumber company was chosen, eight rooms, two storeys, which appeared small to us, but pretentious to our neighbours. It was intended to plaster the house, but there being great difficulty in getting a plasterer, it was decided to use plaster board. This turned out to be the thinnest blue cardboard, a very poor substitute for plaster.

One of the most important projects was to have a well drilled. A driller was engaged, and this man then informed me that I would have to board and feed his crew. I explained this would be impossible, as my house was not yet built. He then told me to get a tent and have a cook stove set up in it, and that his wife would give me a list of provisions and utensils I would require, to prepare and cook the meals. I managed to get the tent and cookstove, and the large supply of food. The Saturday night before work was to commence on the well, one of the drillers saw me at the hotel in Strathmore and said he understood that I was to board the men. He then expressed the hope that I would provide plenty of food, as they were all "good eaters". I told him what I had prepared, and the food that was provided, and then said the only thing that bothered me was how to cook the "beastly stuff". The man replied that he had been a cook in a lumber camp and would undertake to do the cooking, which arrangement suited everybody very well.

An excellent well was drilled which gave us a plentiful supply of water.

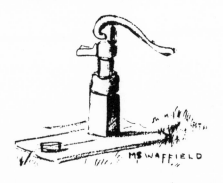

Arrival

These are the Gardens of the Desert, these
The unshorn fields, boundless and beautiful
For which the speech of England has no name.
The Prairies. I behold them for the first
And my heart swells -
　　　William Cullen Bryant - The Prairies

　　It was a beautiful June day, the air crystal
clear and the sky a deeper blue than we had ever
seen in misty England. A gentle little wind
flowed over the prairie, soft and scented. Far
away to the west, beyond the rolling prairie
horizon, we could see the saw-toothed Rockies,
fold on fold of pale blue foothills, rising to
the timber line, then the grey cliffs and crags,
and above all the great snow capped peaks and
glaciers of the high Rockies, the backbone of the
North American continent. The air was so clear
that, although the nearest foothills were almost
a hundred miles away, we could see the
delineation of the folded hills, etched finely
one behind the other.
　　One wonders if anywhere on this planet today,
is air as pure, as sparkling fresh, as it was in
Alberta on that June Day. In the year of 1910
there were few cars, no aeroplanes, and few
industrial plants, between the Great Lakes and
the Pacific Coast, to pollute the air. Later in
the summer during the hot dry days there would be
prairie fires, and the fragrant smell of burning
grass would be carried on the breeze. The
setting sun would then be a deep red, and there
would be a golden haze across the land, but there
was no whiff of smoke in the air on that day.
　　The bright green wagon, with "Massey Harris"
in curly letters angling up the sides, was loaded
high with trunks and baggage. Mother and Father
sat in front on a wooden seat slung from the
wagon sides, and tucked in here and there between
boxes and valises were the five of us and Mary

Ann Bottomley. The twins were sitting side by
side on a trunk, tied securely to a large crate
behind them, bonneted heads bobbing up and down
with the swaying of the wagon, Boppo sat on a box
beside them.

Mother wore a dark green tweed suit, the knee
length jacket, tightly fitted at the waist, and
flared out over the long skirt, the hem of which
swept the ground. Her blouse was cream lace, with
the high neck stiffly boned under each ear, and a
frilly jabot frothing out from her throat. Her
little brown hat, tilted forward, had a brightly
coloured bird-wing at one side, and a spotted
veil, tied round the brim of the hat and usually
knotted under her chin, today was pushed up over
her forehead. Her kid gloved hands were folded on
her lap, and her little purse was of beige
coloured suede with a silver chain handle.

Many years later I found that little purse
among some old treasures in a trunk, and
marvelled at the smallness of it. Women in those
days did not carry compacts, lipsticks, credit
cards, driver's licenses and all the impedimenta
so necessary to us nowadays. Probably a little
embroidered linen handkerchief, a few shillings,
or folded pound notes, and perhaps a tiny silver
topped bottle of smelling salts, would be as much
as mother ever carried with her.

In England, dressing for the occasion was
important in those days. When moving to an new
home a woman would know that neighbours would be
peering curiously from behind Nottingham lace
curtains, tradesmen would be accurately assessing
the class of customer that was moving into his
area, and dress and appearance were important
clues. So today mother was dressed correctly, and
though no neighbours would be watching our
arrival at our new home, no doubt the manager of
the King Edward Hotel, the stationmaster, the
owner of the general store, and the few residents
of the little town of Strathmore had duly
estimated our station in life, and future value
to the community, all from Mother's apppearance.

Betty and I wore our navy blue reefer jackets with the traditional two rows of brass buttons down the fronts, and blue sailor caps with the names of Royal Navy ships printed in gold on the black corded silk bands. Betty's corkscrew curls bobbed and bounced. Her golden-brown hair, so thick and curly, was carefully brushed into twisted curls round Mother's forefinger every morning, and her hair was so well behaved that the curls stayed in all day. My straw coloured hair was straight and wispy, and had no natural curl.

Tommy had a cream coloured coat with an Astrachan collar, and the twins, still babies, wore flanned jackets, one blue, one pink, with palisses, little capes, stitched to the shoulders. Father, already adapted to the garb of the western settler, wore a grey wool flannel shirt, khaki twill trousers, and a large brimmed hat.

I remember watching the twins, rocked by the swaying of the wagon, falling asleep, and slipping sidewise against Boppo, who took one of them on her lap, and put her arm around the other. The little lace trimmed bonnets hung by the ribbons at the back of their necks, and their faces were rosy in the sunlight. Boppo had taken off her hat, and her thick, curly red-gold hair blew gently in the wind. She was twenty two years old, with large blue eyes and a high colour in her cheeks.

She was a happy person, with a dreamy, gentle quality about her, and sometimes there was a faraway look in her eyes that I now know bespoke a secret happiness. She would play games with us, and read us fairy stories when she put us to bed. There was no premonition on that magical day of the tragedy that was to befall her so soon.

The journey from Grandview had been to me, a continuation of the thrilling true life adventure story, which had started the day we left Yeovil, but to my Mother and other older people it must have been a trying experience. We had changed trains at Winnipeg, boarding a crowded colonist train. There was no dining car, the travellers carried their own food with them, and at the end of each car was a small smoky coal stove on which kettles were boiled for tea and coffee. Getting on the train at Winnipeg I had been given a large cocoa tin full of sugar to carry, but I was so bemused and fascinated with all the bustle and confusion, the shouting trainmen, excited children, the great pile of boxes and bundles that were being thrown on the train, that I held the tin upside down, and as we entered the crowded carriage, the lid came off, and the sugar cascaded along the coach floor. As there was no carpet, and the centre aisle was slatted for safety, the sugar could not be swept up and scrunched excruciatingly under every footstep for the whole journey. The travellers had laughed at me, but the harassed trainman scowled, and I squirmed into the farthest corner of a seat, only momentarily embarrassed.

Shortly after leaving Winnipeg we had left the scrubby bush country of Manitoba, and pulled out onto the flat bald headed prairie. As far as the eye could see there was not a tree, nor even a slight rise in the enormous stretch of flat land, that spread endlessly from horizon to horizon, and the sky was a vast clear blue dome that fitted down neatly onto that horizon all around us.

I remember one particularly thrilling event when we saw a herd of antelope that was sailing effortlessly away from the invading monster of the train. The travellers crowded to the windows, excited at the unexpected sight. Once or twice we had stopped at sidings, to allow east bound trains to thunder past, and now and then we pulled into small stations where there were little clusters of men and women on the platforms, with teams and saddle horses tied to hitching posts in the background, and there would be flurries of excitement as mail, freight and baggage were loaded and unloaded.

Eventually we crossed the border from Saskatchewan into Alberta, and here the flat country gave way to the rolling prairie, long sweeping rises that fell away again like enormous ocean swells. From the higher levels we could see vast stretches of country that faded into the blue distance.

At long last the train pulled into the little station at Strathmore, and there was Father waiting for us. He hugged us all, and after gathering up our baggage we crossed the dusty little street to the King Edward Hotel where we stayed the night.

Now on this magical day of our arrival, Bridget and Kate, the Clydesdale mares, pulled the heavy load slowly up the long gradual slope as we headed north. Some miles behind us we could still see the five red grain elevators strung along the railroad at Strathmore. The trail wound across the prairie, two deep ruts made by the wheels of wagons, hayracks and democrats and the hooves of the teams that pulled them, and a shallower rut in the centre made by the single horses, pulling lighter buggies and sulkies. The grass was short, thick and woolly, more grey than green, and the air was scented with wild roses and sweet grass. Gophers popped in and out of their holes, and stood up on their hind legs, their front paws quaintly crossed on their cream coloured tummies, and their noses twitching inquisitively, to watch us pass.

Mother had been convinced that the Canadian prairie was a desolate wasteland, with probably no flowers, nor birds, and of course no trees. The wild roses, a deeper pink than the English dog roses, and so gloriously scented, delighted her. Meadowlarks swooped from buckbrush to buckbrush, trilling their loud, clear song.

Now almost seventy years later, as I look back on that day, every detail of our arrival is clearly defined in my memory. No doubt a child's receptive mind subconsciously observes and records impressions of such new and strange experiences. Everything to me, was so exciting and different to all I had known until that time. At seven years I could appreciate something of what was happening to us, and could sense a little of the reactions of our parents to the many problems and difficulties they were facing.

Betty and I squeezed under the swaying seat and stood up beside Mother's feet, so that we could watch the horses. The great feathered hooves moved slowly and steadily, and little clouds of sandy dust spurted as they lifted and settled into the ruts. Father slapped the reins on the horses' smooth brown rumps, and they leaned into their collars, heads moving up and down rhythmically, heavy black manes lifting and blowing in the breeze.

Tommy, now three and a half years old, sat on the wide swing seat between Mother and Father, her chubby little legs sticking straight out in front of her, and Mother's arm around her. She was the middle child, the odd one out, as Betty and I were inseparable, and of course the twins were too young as yet to play with her. She no doubt was often lonely, but had developed a sure fire way of gaining attention when she felt left out of anything. She merely opened her mouth and roared. Her blue eyes would blaze with the fury of frustration, and the deep, resonant bellow brought all within sound of her to her side immediately. She must have discovered this strategy very early in life, as before we moved to Canada, Mother's sister, Aunt Joy, had nicknamed her "The Bull of Bashan". Directly Tommy's roar had resulted in her receiving the attention she wished, everybody wide-eyed with consternation, she was immediately all gentle and sweet again, and all this without a single tear.

Now, ahead of us the great sweep of prairie rose slowly towards the sky. There was not a tree in sight. On the crest of the rise stood two small buildings, stark and lonely against the sky, and as we drew nearer we could see that they were built of sod, with roofs made of poles covered with straw like untidy thatchings. There was no sign of human or animal life, nor any cultivation around them. Father pulled the horses to a stop. The midday sun was hot now, and he pushed the wide brimmed straw hat to the back of his head. Mother had unbuttoned her jacket and taken off her kid gloves.

"There, Edith! What do you think of that?" Mother sat silently for a minute, and we all stared at the shacks. Suddenly Mother relaxed, and turned to Father, her fringed green eyes full of laughter.

"For a minute I thought - Oh, Harry! If I didn't know you so well, I would have been horrified. Does anybody live there?"

"This piece of prairie belongs to a young Englishman, and a kind American couple who are homesteading further west, helped him build this little sod house and the stable where he keeps his saddle horse. He does sleep here, but is working for farmers in the district, to earn enough money to purchase animals and implements, and then to bring his bride out from Dorset."

"Well, let's hope he can soon provide her a better home than that!" Mother said gently. Father had brought out the young homesteader's mail and papers, and he now climbed down from the wagon, pushed open the wooden door in the sod wall, and laid the bundle on the floor inside. Betty and I leaned over the side of the wagon, peering curiously into the dark interior, and I thought how marvellously exciting it would be to live in the strange little hut.

Our parents took a special interest in this young man, and in the next few months he came to Radfords from time to time, asking advice and help, and he seemed lonely and discouraged. I do not remember his surname, but I believe his first name was Gavin. I can visualize him sitting in the lamplight with his elbows on the kitchen table, as he talked to Mother and Father. He was about twenty five years old, medium height and slight, certainly not the strong, rugged type for prairie pioneer farming, and his slim, fine boned hands were calloused and blistered. He sat rubbing them gently together, as if they were sore and aching.

Some time later he disappeared. A neighbour for whom he had worked, rode over one day to ask if Father knew where he was. The sod shack was emptied of his personal things, but the few pieces of rough hand made furniture were still there. Later it was discovered, that he had ridden into Strathmore one day, put his saddled horse in the livery stable and walked away. It was thought that he might have taken the train, which was due at about that time, up to Calgary, but he was never heard from again. In time the shack collapsed, as the sod disintegrated in the rain and frost, and gradually the grass grew over the mound.

I hope he returned to Dorset, married his fiancee, survived the Great War and lived a comfortable and happy life to the end of his days.

We crested the rise and continued on a level stretch for a couple of miles, then the land sloped away again and we looked out over a wide panorama of gently undulating prairie. We could see signs of life now, little groups of buildings here and there, some fencing, brown squares of ploughed land and patches of green. Here and there were small sloughs, now full with the spring rains, and far away to the right was a sheet of gleaming water. In time to come we learned that this was called Goose Lake, and the wild geese and ducks in thousands used it as a stop-over, on their migrations south in the fall, and north in the spring. In winter when the lake was frozen over, if it wasn't too cold and if there wasn't too much snow, we used it as a skating rink.

Father pulled the horses to a stop, and we sat in silence for a minute as we gazed out over the wide vista. In the distance, to the north east, the land rose again into low, rounded, bare hills, and from behind us the western sun poured its golden rays across the landscape. Two or three miles ahead was a little knoll, smooth and bare, and on the top of this we could see a square building, the unpainted wood shining yellow in the sunshine. Father took the whip out of its socket and without a word pointed it towards the distant mound.

"Is that it?" Mother said quietly.

"That's it". There was no joking in Father's voice this time, and he turned anxiously to see Mother's reaction."It doesn't look much from here and of course it isn't finished. When it's painted and has a few trees about it, and then we can add a verandah, and stables and chicken houses will go up behind, then a garden, and all neatly fenced - " Father's voice faltered. "I am afraid it will be pretty primitive living for a while, Edith. No running water, no plumbing, no gas for cooking."

"We'll manage, Harry." She turned her head towards him, and put her hand on his, "Others are making a go of it." Mother spoke cheerfully but she was not smiling. She had been anticipating this moment for a long time, and no doubt the realization was a bit of a shock. "We'll call it Radfords! That will make it seem more like home."

This was to be the third "Radfords" in Mother's lifetime. The first, near Dawlish in Devonshire, had been the home of her family for generations, an L-shaped Elizabethan house, with a low thatched roof, and floors of heavy oaken boards that wavered up and down. The second, had been the large red brick house in Yeovil, built for them before Mother and Father were married, and where their five children had been born.

The arrival of the family at the newest Radfords must have been something of an anticlimax. As the tired horses pulled the loaded wagon up the rutted track to the house, we saw many large packing cases and boxes of belongings piled, still unopened, about the house, and left over pieces of lumber, shingles, rolls of black tar paper, and all kinds of rubbish scattered about. The house which had looked quite lovely from the rise some miles away, standing four square on top of the little rounded hill, and outlined against the blue rolling prairie behind it, now appeared rather lonely and pathetic. Looking to the north and east as we approached, not a sign of habitation or human life could be seen, the country vacant and empty to the far horizon.

A small tent stood among the packing cases, and as we drew up to the house a short elderly man pushed the flap open and came out. He staggered slightly as he shuffled towards us. I recognized him as the carpenter who had worked for the Holman family, on their farm at Grandview, when we arrived there three months earlier, and who had joined Father, and travelled west with him to help build the house.

Father climbed stiffly down over the front wheel and stood watching him as he stumbled through the packing cases and debris towards us. His clothes were bedraggled, his spiky hair stood out in all directions, and his bushy mustache drooped forlornly.

"Lane, I thought you were going to have all this stuff unpacked and sorted out for us by this time. What happened?" The sad looking little man shook his head and pulled at the long taggles of his mustache.

"Couldn't help it, Mr. Petter, had an awful headache when I got up this morning. Had to lie down all day. I'll get right at it in the morning."

"That won't do, Lane, we need the bedding and some dishes and other necessities for the night. Try and find the boxes of bedding first." He turned back to the wagon and helped Mother and Boppo down, and Mr. Lane shambled off. Father smiled at Mother, who was looking rather shaken.

"Should have checked his tent for the bottle of whisky before I left yesterday. He'll pull himself together, and unpack enough for the night. Don't worry, Edith !"

Of course I did not hear this conversation at the time. Betty and I had already jumped down from the wagon and were busy exploring, but I did hear it repeated from time to time over the following years.

Inside the house was untidy and littered, far from finished, and smelled strongly of half seasoned wood. The partitions between the rooms were made of plasterboard nailed onto the joists, and this plasterboard was not much more than thick, felty paper, one could push one's finger through it. The floors and ceilings were rough, unplaned boards, and in time to come, we found that if one walked or ran on the bare boards without shoes on, one's feet were soon full of agonizing splinters, requiring somebody's immediate attention with tweezers, and bowls of boiling water laced with boracic acid, to prevent blood poisoning.

A large black cook stove stood in the kitchen and a roughly made table and wooden kitchen chairs were all the furniture on the main floor. Upstairs, bedsteads had been set up in the bedrooms, with mattresses laid on them, but with as yet, of course no bedding.

I remember little of the rest of that eventful day, and the nights and days that followed. We must have lived a sort of gypsy life, camping in the unfinished house and unfurnished rooms. The unpacking of the huge crates of furniture and other necessities went on for some time. Shiny brown cork linoleum was laid over the rough floor boards, and gradually the house became liveable.

The supply of bread brought out from Strathmore, ran out very soon, and Mr. Lane, who the day after our arrival had completely recovered from his little lapse, and from then on was wonderfully helpful, showed Mother how to make bannock in a frying pan. We had hot bannock for every meal! Father had laid in a large supply of canned food before we arrived and of course that helped - large cans of stewed tomatoes, flat oval tins of smoked herring and cans of salmon. Sides of bacon and large hams were hung from the rafters in the cellar, which was just a hole in the ground under the house. Father had bought a cow, which was housed in a rough shed, with a small corral behind it, so we had a good supply of fresh milk.

One of the blessings, as the days became hotter, was the ice cold water that was pumped, by hand of course, from the deep well, which had been drilled by a well-digging outfit while the house was being built. The water was very hard, which made the washing of clothes and dishes difficult, with only soap to work with, no detergents or water softeners in 1910. Later, water barrels were set under the eavestroughs, and the frequent thunderstorms kept them filled with soft rainwater. This was carried into the kitchen in pails, and heated in the large side-boiler on the cookstove, and the copper wash boiler. In winter, snow was packed into washtubs, hauled into the back kitchen to melt, and then heated.

A new World - a new home - a new life - a life so different and so demanding of the inexperienced men and women, but to the children adventuresome and exciting. I have many happy, but some sad, memories of the following eight years on the Alberta Prairie.

The New Radfords

Harry Petter had promised his wife that the new Radfords would be as nearly as possible, a replica of the handsome red brick Yeovil house, but apart from having three storeys, so unsuitable for the windswept, bald prairie - it was a poor imitation. The rooms were smaller, although there were the same number on the main floor, a hall, a dining room, "drawing room", kitchen, and back kitchen, and four bedrooms on the second floor. The third storey, which in the original, contained the servant's bedrooms, was merely a windowless attic under the roof, and was reached by a ladder through a trap door. There was no bathroom, as of course there was no running water or plumbing, the bedrooms had no clothes' closets and there was no roomy linen cupboard, or the traditional larder off the kitchen. Our clothing hung on the bedroom walls from nails hammered into the wooden joists.

The clapboard exterior was eventually painted red, but no paint can duplicate the soft rosy red of bricks. The walls were all lined with tarpaper, but the first winter we soon found out they couldn't keep out the cold, when the blizzards started sweeping across the open prairie. The thin, black stovepipes, with many elbows, rose from the kitchen range and the Nautilus heater in the sitting room, through the ceilings into the bedrooms, and on up into the attic, and through the shingled roof. The fuel used was mainly the soft surface coal from the Red Deer Valley, and this soon formed a very flammable accumulation of creosote in the elbows in the pipes. Time and again there would be furious chimney fires when the pipes would glow red hot. Somebody would scream "Chimney's on fire!" and buckets of water would be rushed to the nearest floor in case the fire burned through the metal and set fire to the walls.

The Yeovil Radfords had had a large garden,

surrounded by ornamental trees and shrubs and
flower beds, in front, a smooth green lawn,
and tennis court, and behind the house was a
brick-walled kitchen garden and fragrant herb
bed. At first the new Radfords sat starkly on its
rounded hillock with no garden and not a tree or
shrub in sight, other than a few low clumps of
buckbrush here and there around the badger holes.
A year or two later a windbreak of young trees
purchased from the C.P.R. Experimental Farm at
Strathmore was planted around the house, poplars,
willows, and some hardy evergreens, and they in
time grew sufficiently to help break the winds,
but at first our new home stood out for miles
like a sore thumb.

Leading up from the hall inside the front
door, was a steep, narrow staircase. Half way up
this was a right angled turn and a little
landing, and off this a narrow passage led into a
little storeroom. Climbing the stairs on a dark
winter's night on our way to bed, with the wind
howling ouside, and carrying a flickering candle
or smoky, dim kerosene lantern, passing that dark
little opening was a terrifying experience.
Goodness knew what horror could be crouching in
the darkness, ready to grab us as we slipped
past, squeezing ourselves against the opposite
wall.

Soon after our arrival, with the cheerful
help of Mr. Lane (we never knew if he had a first
name, he was always "Mr. Lane" to us), a horse
barn with four stalls was built at the bottom of
the slope on the east side of the house, and
later a cowshed was built onto one side of it.
Father was soon out introducing himself to the
earlier settlers in the district, gleaning much
helpful advice and information, and acquiring
stock and farm equipment. He would come home
with a cow tied to the back of his buggy, a
couple of pigs, or a crate of fowl. So pig styes
had to be constructed below the barn, and then a
sod henhouse, with a sloping roof, of chickenwire
covered with straw, was built.

Some fifty yards or so from the house was a little square building with a pointed, shingled roof. It stood off by itself, stiff and square, and rather like a sentry-box, and it sat on top of a deep hole. This was the outside toilet, or the "Little House", as it was called. The narrrow, tall door, which was placed coyly on the side away from the house and its windows, had a small diamond shaped aperture in its upper half. Inside, a seat was built across the back wall, with two smoothly sanded oval shaped holes. Beside the seat, a length of hooked wire was hung on a nail on the wall, and square pieces of paper, cut from old newspapers, catalogues, and magazines, were speared onto it. On the floor, was a large box of sandy soil, with a small scoop, and a couple of shovels full of soil were poured through the holes in the seat by each user in turn. From time to time a new hole would be dug, the Little House moved over on to it, and the old hole filled in.

Later when Radfords itself was painted its deep red, the little outside toilet was also painted to match, and in time a well worn path curved across the grass, from the house and round to the door at the back. Mr. Lane added a clever invention of his own. He attached, to the corner of the Little House by the door, a wooden lever, which could be swivelled out like a warning hand, or a railway signal, and this could be seen from the house to notify all that the Little House was occupied.

My memories of the following eight years that our family spent on the Strathmore farm are like a jumbled drawerful of old photos - I pick them out at random, now from the difficult but exciting early years, now from a later period, winter or summer, spring or fall; now a gay one, then one touched with sadness or remorse. Yes, remorse! myself, hiding for hours in the stable loft, tucked comfortably in the fragrant hay, reading Swiss Family Robinson, or Lorna Doone, instead of assisting Mother with the endless household chores; pretending to be ill so that I wouldn't have to help with the milking, or feed the pigs. But many of these flashbacks are to do with the precious little family jokes, and gaieties, that remain safely stored in my memory, and will be, hopefully, to the end of my days.

Those years must have been a struggle, and an enormous challenge for our parents, so unused to the problems and difficulties of pioneer life on the prairie, but to my sisters and myself they were crammed with delightful excitements, joyful adventures, wonderful games in the barns and straw piles, picnics at the "meteorite", that strange great granite rock that lay in solitary splendor on a grassy slope a few miles from Radfords, and which was undoubtedly deposited there by some melting glacier in ages long past. We had read about meteorites, comets, and shooting stars, in our well illustrated Childrens' Books of Knowledge, and decided that the great stone must be a meteorite. There were tea parties out in the hayfields, and long rides, often bareback, cantering over the beautiful, rolling prairie which in those years was mostly as untouched by man as it had been since its beginning.

Only as I have grown older, in retrospect, have I fully realized the loneliness and homesickness of our parents, and the strength and determination that carried them through. Then we children only thought of our own happy days, and if we were at all conscious of the trials and tribulations of the grownups, it was only a passing reflection from which we could quickly turn away.

I shall take out a memory here, and a memory there, and get as much as possible down on paper as it comes to me, so that I can be sure that in the years to come, that which is clear in my mind today, will not disappear into the mists of time.

I can see Mother hurrying across the barnyard, her long woollen skirt almost covering the heavy leather boots she wore outdoors, and

closely followed wherever she went, by a train of
downy yellow ducklings in tight formation, at her
heels. These no doubt would have been hatched by
a broody hen, who would have had no idea how to
provide food for ducks - and of course Mother
would have had to take on that responsibilty,
with the result that the ducklings looked on her
as their lawful parent, and provider of meals. She
tenderly called them her "Little de'ils".

Another flashback - Father up hours before
daybreak in the dark, bitter winter mornings to
start fires in the kitchen stove, and the iron
heaters, to make "summer" as he jokingly called
it, in the house, so that the bedrooms would be
warm for us to dress in.

One very happy memory - Daddy and I, with
Bridget and Kate hitched to the wagon, driving to
the Bannister Ranch some twenty or so miles west
of us, to buy oats for seed. We left before sunup
on a crisp spring morning, the Rockies standing
up blue and sharp against the translucent western
sky. Soon they would be touched with rose and
gold, as the sun tipped the horizon behind us. We
bought ·a loaf of doughy white bread and a jar of
marmalade at Cheadle, to top off the meat
sandwiches we had brought with us for lunch. How
good it all tasted! We ate sitting on a bank
covered with purple prairie crocuses, while the
horses rested and munched their oat sheaves.

Late in the afternoon we came to the cutbanks
of the Bow River, and as we followed the winding
trail down a gully we could see the ranch house
and farm building of the Bannister Ranch spread
out on the river flats below us. It was exciting
to see real trees again, trees with great twisted
trunks, Garry Oaks, the nobby leaf buds still
unopened, and feathery aspens and poplars, just
breaking into leaf, shimmering in the golden,
afternoon sunlight. Beyond, the Bow itself, in
full spring spate, and as brilliantly blue as the
sky above, wound through the valley. Far to the
west, the snows and glaciers of the Rockies were
melting, and the ice cold, crystal clear water

was tearing down the rivers and creeks across the prairies.

The Bannisters came out to meet us as we drove up the trail to the front of the large log cabin. Two handsome dogs sniffed round the wagon and wagged their tails in greeting. We were invited in, and made so very welcome. Unexpected guests were always welcome in those days on the lonely farms and ranches as they brought news of the outside world, and gossip of neighbours, at a time when there were, of course, no telephones, and mail and newspapers were often not picked up for weeks on end.

There was always a plentiful supply of eggs, milk and butter, home cured ham and bacon, bread and bannock, and most farm wives could cope with an extra three or four hungry men at short notice. Many a luckless fowl or duck, would have its neck wrung, skin and feathers stripped off, and be popped into the frying pan or pot before it had had time to cool.

We stayed the night, and after a fine breakfast, started for home again while the morning was still young. The wagon had been loaded the night before, and Father bought another team of horses from the rancher, a strong pair of geldings, and these were to pull the heavy wagon with the mares tied to the tailgate.

It was a long slow drive home, and darkness had fallen while we still had a few miles to go. The stars came out, and I lay on top of the oats, listening to Father singing "Can't you hear the wagons as the wheels roll along?","Nellie Gray", "Drink to me Only with Thine Eyes" and "A Bicycle Built for Two", in his clear strong voice.

Staring up at the enormous dome of black sky, the stars seemed to swim and jerk, as the wagon lurched over the rutted trail. Mother had put a lighted oil lamp in the diningroom window, as she always did when Father was coming home after dark, and we could see the faint spark as we topped the rise, still several miles from home.

Before - the five sisters at
        Radfords, Yeovil, England.

After - the five sisters at
        Radfords, Strathmore, Alberta.

Joan and Betty "riding" at Radfords, England.

Joan and Betty riding Nick at Radfords, Canada.

Status Symbols and Mixed Blessings

The English colonists of those days must have provoked many a chuckle from the earlier more hardened pioneers by their attempt, often so inappropriate, to carry on with their traditional way of life. At that time out on the prairie it was considered a form of snobbishness to have a "drawing room", a piano, or to call the midday meal luncheon, instead of dinner.

Thinking back to those days, I have come to realize, that the stubborn and sometimes even ridiculous refusal of the English newcomers to adapt to the rough-and-ready, but practical way of life, on what was then the "frontier", was not so much to impress their neighbours, as an attempt to keep up their own courage, and to assure themselves that they would not lose touch with their old way of life, that there was hope that someday all the traditional customs and comforts they had left behind, would be theirs once more.

Except for breakfast, our meals during the first few months were eaten in the diningroom on white linen tablecloths, smoothly laid on the round oak table, with linen serviettes beside each place, and a bowl of wild flowers in the centre. As heretofore, Father carved the joint, and Mother served the vegetables. After our Boppo's sad death and as times grew harder and help more difficult to find, Mother came to accept the thick white oilcloth tablecloth which could be left on the big kitchen table day and night, and which could be wiped clean with a sweep of the dishcloth. Food was dished directly out of the saucepans onto the plates, and soon meals in the diningroom were rare, and only on special occasions, as when the Rector of St. Michael and All Angels, in Strathmore, made his formal calls.

But we had our drawingroom. It was a fair-sized, oblong room with two large windows

hung with the rose patterned chintz curtains that
had come out with us, and the large black upright
piano, with its two brass candlesticks on the
front panel, stood against the wall. Father had
taken apart one of the old Jacobean oak chests,
and rebuilt it into a sort of mantelpiece which
surrounded the Nautilus heater in one corner, and
it made a handsome substitute for a real
fireplace. On the oilcloth covered floor were
laid five fluffy sheepskin rugs, which had been
bought from the McLean's sheep ranch on the
Serviceberry Creek, and the comfortable sofa and
armchairs which had furnished our Yeovil drawing
room fitted in nicely.

The drawingroom opened off the little hall,
close to the front door, and in the spring,
before the screen door went up to keep out the
swarming mosquitoes and flies, this door was
often open to the farmyard, in which at that time
our animals, chickens, ducks and geese roamed at
will. One day Mother returned from a trip to
town, glanced into the drawingroom, as she
entered the front door with her arms full of
parcels, and saw five half grown pigs stretched
out, one on each of the sheepskin rugs, sleeping
peacefully.

On the opposite side of the front door, the
staircase led up to the bedrooms, and under the
bottom step was an opening where a board had
slipped out. We called the small dark space into
which we could peer, the "Thump-a-lump", probably
because the step above it groaned eerily when
walked on. We invented ghost stories about the
Thump-a-lump and found it a useful place into
which we could throw overshoes, mitts, scarves or
anything that we did not need at the moment.

We had a pet hen we called "Crouchie",
because she would crouch down beside anybody who
happened to be sitting out on the front steps,
and carry on a long monologue of soft chirrups
and gurgles, deep in her throat. Mother was fond
of the big, handsome Buff Orpington, and when
"Crouchie" was sitting beside her, Mother would

stroke her neck and back. Crouchie discovered the Thump-a-lump, and if she could slip in the front door, would creep in and lay a large brown egg among the discarded wool caps and mitts.

Our most prestigious status symbol during that first year, one which at that time was unique in the area, we acquired a few months after our arrival - a real bathtub. Father had never been able to accustom himself to curling up, knees to chin, in the round galvanized washtub, in front of the kitchen range. The new tub was ordered from Eaton's Department Store in Winnipeg and was shipped to us by freight in a large wooden crate. The tub was of heavy metal, enameled white inside, and dark green outside, and had four splayed feet. As we had no bathrooom, it had to sit in a corner of the kitchen, and of course had no hot and cold faucets, there being no hot nor cold running water. However, Father did attach a pipe to the plug and let it down through the floor to the yard outside, to allow the bathwater to run away. The water had to be heated on the range, in the copper wash boiler, and carried across to the bath in buckets, but nobody minded that. A wooden cover was made to fit over the top of the bath, and this made a useful shelf on which to keep water pails, milk buckets, and other kitchen gadgets.

During these years our two Uncles, Ernest and Percy, were prospering with the family firm of Petter Engines in Yeovil, England and a year or two after we settled in Alberta, out of the kindness of their hearts, they shipped out to Father a small, stationary, all-purpose oil engine, for use on the farm.

This proved to be a great help, but also a mixed blessing. As soon as the engine arrived, Father bought a fanning mill, which the engine would run, to clean oats and wheat, and which also chopped oats for feed, and turned our home grown wheat into fine brown flour.

This little engine was a great novelty at

that time, of course, and farmers came from near and far to inspect it and watch it running the efficient mill, pumping water from our deep well for the stock, and for the house. Father was very proud of the whole outfit, and kept promising this neighbour and that, to chop a load of oats,or grind a few sacks of flour. It was taken for granted that Father would be paid, of course, but somehow nobody seemed able to pay at the time, and Father was so proud, and pleased to be showing off his prime acquisition, that he could never bring himself to mention money, no matter how many mornings or afternoons he spent grinding and fanning and chopping, or how much oil he used up doing these favours. Mother would say:

"Harry, have you reminded Mr. So and So that he promised to pay you for chopping those two wagon loads of oats?" and Father would answer:

"Oh, I could never do that, my dear. I wouldn't embarrass the poor man to that extent for anything!"

M.S.

Sauerkraut and Baloney

Downey and Salmon were the proprietors of the General Store in Strathmore in 1910, and to the new settlers, shopping at their emporium was a voyage of discovery. One could learn a lot about the needs of pioneer life in those days, just by poking about in the dark, crowded interior. Hundred pound cotton bags of flour and sugar, were piled from floor to ceiling, huge brown sacks of oatmeal, great wheels of yellow cheese, and wooden buckets of plum and apple jam, were stacked along the floor, and on the counters. There were no small neat packages of food in those days, everything was in large quantities. There were wooden tubs of vinegary sauer-kraut, barrels of pickled herring, and a row of large square tin boxes full of a great assortment of "cookies", biscuits to us. These boxes, with the lids off, were on a stand that tipped them sidewise, so that the shoppers could make their choice. Our favourite cookie was a large, round, flat biscuit piled high with rubbery marshmallow, brilliant pink, chocolate or white, thickly covered with flaked cocoanut. Delicious!

There were bolts of material, sewing supplies, piles of underwear, grey wool blankets, flannelette sheets, trousers, sheepskin lined jackets, straw hats, woollen socks, long black ribbed stockings, and a multitude of other things piled here and there.

Across the one short block of dusty main street, was a butcher shop, and here in summertime, the butcher waged a battle with the swarms of voracious bluebottles. The sides and quarters of beef, mutton and pork that hung in rows on each side of the little shop were draped in butter muslin. There were slabs of salt pork and bacon, and strangest of all to us, the great tubes of red "baloney" encased in shiny cotton canvas.

There was no bakery, bread could be bought at

Downey and Salmons', but it was queer stuff, soft and doughy, and so white that father said it must be made of plaster-of-paris. When you tried to cut it, it collapsed into a doughy lump. Our favourite bread in Yeovil had been a "cottage loaf", a large round loaf with a smaller round top and a hole down through the middle of both, poked by the baker with his finger before it was baked, to hold the two together. It was firm, but porous, and could be sliced paper thin, then well buttered for the plates of "bread and butter" that were always on the English tea tables.

It was all so different! The farmer's wife had to plan her supplies for weeks ahead, especially in winter when the blizzards would isolate the farms for long periods, or during harvest or haying, when everybody was far too busy to make the often long drive into town with wagon or buggy. There were no convenient little shops just around the corner, no baker's boy calling every morning before breakfast, to deliver fresh baked bread and hot rolls,(buns, they were called in England). No butcher's boy at the back door, in his long blue and white striped apron with little black book, to take your orders. Milk and groceries, fruit and vegetables, were delivered daily at your kitchen door, in England in those days.

Except what could be grown on the farms, fresh vegetables and fruit were scarce, and only obtainable in season, on the prairies at that time. There was no refrigeration of course, and so shipping and storing fresh produce in the hot weather was difficult, and it was often over ripe or rotten, when it arrived at its destination. In winter it might freeze solid between station and store. We depended a good deal on dried fruit, and I remember the wooden crates of prunes, raisins, currants, and dried apple rings, that were ordered from Eaton's Winnipeg store, and which were shipped to us by train. The prunes and apple rings were packed in neat rows, and jammed down so tightly that it was difficult to pry them loose. The apple rings were hard, and brown, and had to be soaked for hours before being cooked. The raisins were not seeded, and it was one of my jobs to "stone" them for cakes, scones and raisin pies. Naturally, quite a few would be popped into my mouth during the process, and that unfortunate thievery was to bring retribution down on my head, and much worry and expense to my poor parents in time to come.

Some canned food was available, but Mother was suspicious of cans, we had heard rumours of people being poisoned by poorly canned meat. Canned salmon and large tins of seedy tomatoes were used in emergencies, the salmon was pale pink and watery, and many little wheels of vertebrae floated in the juice.

Flapjacks were a popular standby, a delicious new experience to us. They were very different to the paper thin pancakes rolled in sugar, and served with lemon juice, that we always had had on Shrove Tuesday. Flapjacks were large and thick, fried golden brown, and served with plenty of butter, and dollops of real maple syrup. They made breakfast, and sometimes suppers, fit for kings.

One of the greatest problems facing the women folk of the new settlers during that spring and summer of 1910, was the shortage of fuel with which to stoke the iron cookstoves. Later in the fall the men would drive the forty miles to Carbon, on the Red Deer River, for coal, but during the summer they were too busy building barns and sheds, ploughing the summer-fallow for the following spring planting, cutting hay, and caring for the stock. There were no mossy woods in which we could gather faggots, as we might have done in Somerset. The children were kept busy scrounging scraps of lumber left over by the carpenters, but the dry wood burned up quickly and produced little heat. Somehow meals had to be cooked for the hungry men and children, and there seemed no immediate solution to the difficulty.

One afternoon, shortly after we arrived at

the new Radfords, we saw a one-horse buggy approaching across the prairie. It reached our gate, and a tall woman in a long gingham dress and a large straw hat, stepped down, tied the horse to a fence post, and walked up to the house. I watched her as she approached, and she smiled at us as we gazed up at her, fascinated because she was the first woman visitor we had had. She had blue eyes which looked strangely pale in her wide sunburned face, and her thick greying hair was pulled back into a large bun, on which the flat straw hat rested. Mother came out and greeted her, and the two women went into the house.

This woman was an American, recently widowed, and she was visiting her sister and brother-in-law who were farming in the Rockyford area. She was a born frontiers-woman. She and her family had pioneered to the American west in her childhood, and so she had ready answers to many of the problems, that seemed insurmountable to the English newcomers. She drove over to Radfords several times in the following days, taught Mother and Boppo how to make bread, how to cure bacon and ham, and showed them in many ways how to make housekeeping and cooking easier, with the primitive resources available at that time, but most important of all, she had a solution for the lack of fuel.

There were many miles of open prairie to the east and south of us at that time, and the range cattle roamed over it in great numbers. Mrs. Lindquist told us that the "cowpats", the round flat cakes of manure that were thickly scatterd everywhere on the open plains, dry and hard under the hot sun and drying winds, made a fuel not unlike peat. Purely digested grass, with the moisture dried out of them, they were odorless except for the faint fragrance of burning grass, when the stove lid was lifted, and the red-hot bed of glowing fuel stirred with the iron poker.

Later Mother learned from her brother, Jack Pardon, who had emigrated to South Africa a year or two before we left for Canada, that the Boers of the great Veldts burned dried cow dung for stove fuel and called it "schou". So we had a name for this most useful natural resource!.

After the first year we grew our own potatoes and they flourished in the rich prairie soil, growing fast in the hot days and nights of late spring and summer, and with ample moisture from the frequent thunderstorms. However, harvesting them before the early frosts, and storing them where they woud not freeze, were problems. By the end of August we could expect a heavy frost any night, and getting in the grain crops was, of course, the first priority for the farmers. The potatoes often had to wait until the middle of September, or later. Then the long rows were turned over by the hand plough, and the potatoes scattered out over the frost rimmed furrows. They had to be picked up, thrown into sacks and loaded onto a stoneboat, then covered with sacks as quickly as possible to prevent their freezing. We all helped with this, and it was often bitterly cold work. Our hands would be numb, as we scrabbled up the fine, large potatoes from the icy soil, but we made a sort of game out of it, vying with each other as to who would find the biggest potato. We stored ours under the house, in the big, dark cellar, but some farmers stored their root crops in deep dug-outs, with mounds of soil thrown up over them, and a small opening at each end for ventilation.

Some of the slightly frozen potatoes were salvaged that first fall, and we found out what frozen potatoes tasted like when cooked. Horrible! The starch content turns to a form of sugar and when boiled the potatoes turn into a gluey , sticky mess that is quite uneatable.

During that autumn Father heard that a farmer some miles south of Strathmore, who had a fine crop of cabbages, was selling them. So Father drove over with a wagon and team, and eventually found this farm. Late that night, he arrived back with a wagonful of large green cabbages, which he had bought for 10 cents a head, but it had not occurred to him that storing a winter's supply might be a problem. The farmer had warned him not to store them in bins as they would rot. The cabbages still had an inch or two of thick stalk, so Father punched holes through the stalks, strung them on bindertwine, then hung them in long loops under the floor joists in the cellar, and in the dim light of the hurricane lantern, they gleamed like pearl necklaces. In due course, the outer leaves dried into stiff papery casings, and the insides bleached pure white, but they still tasted like cabbages, and they lasted us all winter.

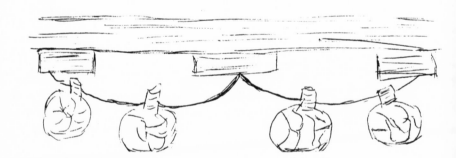

The Prairie Bible

On the prairie farms and ranches in the early years of this century the arrival of Eaton's catalogue was a very important event that everybody looked forward to with cheerful anticipation. It was certainly the most popular well studied book in the isolated homes, where opportunities to shop in the cities came seldom. The "Spring and Summer" and "Fall and Winter" issues would arrive from Winnipeg by post, and would be thumbed through from first page to last by every member of each household.

Clothing, sheepskin lined coats, thick felt boots, buffalo robes, cream separators, bread mixers, stone hot water bottles, wooden churns, furniture, farm machinery, wagons, buggies, harness - every imaginable need would be found in the large, thick book. The pages of toys, games and books were naturally the most popular with children, and we spent many hours studying them, and happily choosing what we wanted for birthdays and Christmas. Eaton's famous Beauty Doll was always the favourite with girls, and the child who received one was much envied by the others. Betty, who was more interested in dolls than Barbara or I, was the lucky one in our family, and she dearly loved and cherished it. I believe it cost three or four dollars, a large sum for a toy at that time, but the doll was a work of art, with a china head and body, jointed arms and legs, real hair, eyes that opened and shut and handsomely dressed. (In the Christmas Gift flyer from Eaton's of 1981 a replica of this doll is shown and priced at $400.00, a collector's item now.)

In the last section of the catalogue would be listed every kind of food, flour and sugar by the hundredweight, packed in coarse white cotton sacks, oatmeal, dried fruits, tinned goods, and household needs such as soaps, cleaners and all sorts of medications. Long lists would be made out on the order forms and sent off. In due course the orders would arrive by freight from Winnipeg, hauled out by wagon or sleigh to the ranches or farms, where unpacking the large wooden boxes was almost as exciting as opening parcels on Christmas morning.

When a new catalogue arrived, the old issue would be grabbed by the children to be used for a favourite game, "cutting out". From the clothing section, figures of women would be cut out, then matching dresses and coats, hats and even boots and shoes, would be carefully snipped with little tabs here and there around the edges, to fold over the figure. In time one could arrange a whole wardrobe of different styles, and many hours of a long winter's day would be happily occupied. Then, the final ultimate destiny of this valuable piece of pioneer lifestyle, was when the remaining pages were carefully cut into fours, the squares speared by the corners onto a piece of hooked wire, and eventually the lot hung on a nail in the little house that stood off by itself in the farmyard.

To those farm women whose lives prior to emigrating to the Canadian prairie had been spent in towns or cities, and who had been able to shop for their clothes in person, it must have been a real deprivation to have to depend on ordering by mail. The nearest dress shops to us were in Calgary, and that meant a long drive into Strathmore, then a two hour train journey and a one or two day stay in Calgary. It would be a rare occasion when a busy farm wife would be able to spare the time, and afford the cost of making the trip.

In the year 1909 when our family was still living in Yeovil, and I was six years old, one of my special treats had been to go shopping with Mother. On quiet, golden summer afternoons or crisp winter mornings when hoar frost sparkled on the bare branches of the trees, or on autumn days when the joyful wind sent showers of leaves swirling around us, we would walk down the tree bordered Avenue from Radfords to the Borough, the shopping centre of the town. Fine red brick houses with tidy flower beds and smooth green lawns bordered the Avenue, and it was along its white pavements that Betty and I would often run, bowling our wooden hoops on the way to Grandmother's house across the Park, for lessons with Aunt Eva.

On the shopping days Mother and I would call in at one of the little dress shops, and I would sit on a stool and watch her being shown lovely gowns, and handsome coats, by an attentive shop woman. Then, having chosen something, she was fitted by the seamstress, who always wore a long, black sateen apron with a tape measure hanging round her neck, and who had her mouth full of pins.

However, the real highlight of these expeditions would be when Mother decided she needed a new hat. The millinery shop was on the opposite side of the Borough, and one or two especially handsome hats would be displayed on stands in the small, leaded glass window, straws and silks in summer, beavers and felts in winter. Inside would be large, summery straw hats with massed arrangements of flowers clustered over the crown, furry beavers, with colourful birdwings or sweeping ostrich plumes, gorgeous velvet toques with brilliant sequins sewn over them, and there would be dozens of spotted or patterned gauzy veils to go with the hats.

All the hats were made by hand in a little room behind the shop, and I would slip in and watch the young woman working there, sometimes sewing yards of woven inch wide straw strips, some as fine as lace, into summer hats. She would start in the middle of the crown, then work round and round, manipulating the strips to shape the crown, then spreading it wider and wider to form the brim. When it was finished and the crown lined with silk, large golden daisies and scarlet poppies might be sewn round the band to make a lovely creation.

On our way home, if it happened to be at the
end of the month, Mother would stop at the
grocer's to pay the monthly bill. He would be
standing behind the counter in his starched white
apron, with his shiny black hair plastered flat
over his forehead, and after mother had paid him
with pound notes out of her purse, he would smile
at me, and leaning over the counter hand me a
little white box of chocolates.

Joan , with her hoop.

Prairie Bounty

FLOWERS, MUSHROOMS, WILD STRAWBERRIES

In spring and summer, during our first years at Radfords, the wild flowers were a never ending pleasure. There was still much unfenced range land to the east and south, for there the soil had not been disturbed by plough or shovel since time began, and the succession of nature's prolific glory must have brought much pleasure to the new settlers, especially to those who had left flower filled gardens behind them in their former homes.

The beautiful, mauve prairie crocus, the pasque flower, was pushing its silver grey buds through the ground, before the frost and snow had disappeared. The rolling prairie for as far as the eye could see, would soon be misty blue, with washes of pink and mauve and grey, in sun and shadow, as the warm spring winds wafted the feathery clouds across the sky. Soon the brimming sloughs would be circled with pale pink shooting stars, waving delicately in the fragrant sweet-grass scented breezes. The wild roses were a deeper pink that the English varieties, but perhaps not as sweet-scented as the dogroses and brier roses, that grew in the hedges at home. Then came the tiger lilies, flaming orange and scarlet, and the bright red spears of Indian paint brush. The silver-grey herb that we called "prairie lavender" grew everywhere. It was deliciously aromatic, and Mother dried it as she had dried lavender at home, and put it in the little cotton bags that the table salt came in, to be placed between the sheets and towels.

Later in the summer came the gaillardias, large daisy-like flowers, orange, gold and red with black velvety centres. Black eyed susans waved on tall, slender stems. Still later, the tall, elegant, purple Michaelmas daisies and goldenrod blossomed.

A year or so after we arrived, we had a very warm, wet June, and one morning the range land to the south of us was speckled white with mushrooms. They seemed to have sprung up overnight, and they were the most delicious mushrooms we had ever eaten. Many were already huge, snow white, with the delicate pink frills under the fat caps, just breaking out from the paper-like covering.

In Somerset, England, families would go out into the fields and commons with wicker baskets to pick mushrooms, but they were small, brown and tough, compared with these luscious beauties. Bucketsful were gathered. The sliced mushrooms were fried in butter, and served with bacon or sausages, for breakfasts and suppers. Great pots of creamy mushroom soup bubbled on the cookstove, and Mother made quarts of mushroom ketchup, which was stored in crocks. This surprising bonus, "Manna from Heaven!" said Father, only lasted a couple of days. Then the mushrooms dried up and disappeared, or were eaten by the gophers. In later years patches of mushrooms were found after the spring rains, but never again as far as I can remember, such a crop as in that year.

In the little hollows where the prairie soil was thick and rich and moist, wild strawberries flourished. They were small compared with the cultivated berries, but even better flavoured, and grew so thickly that we could fill a three pound lard pail in a very short time. When not too busy, Mother set pans of milk on which the cream had risen, on the back of the stove to scald, making Devonshire cream. No dessert could be finer than a bowl of wild strawberries with a dollop of Devonshire cream on top.

A few miles to the northeast of Radfords, on the rising ground beyond the Serviceberry Creek, were some strange, round, conical shaped depressions, or pits. They were there seventy years ago, and I presume they are still there, unless the dry seasons in the twenties and thirties, when the dust storms blew for days on end, filled them in with dry drifting soil. They were about fifty or so feet deep, and about the same across. The sides sloped down cleanly from the level ground to the pointed bottoms. There were several of them, identical in shape and size, within an area of one or two acres. We were told that they were ice age potholes. Over the many years the rich humus had been washed down the sides of these "holes", and in the springs of plentiful rain, and hot sunshine, fine crops of wild strawberries grew in the bottom.

Not far from these pot holes, a mile or so to the southeast, in a depression in the side of a coulee, was a large granite rock or stone. It must have weighed many tons, and stood fifteen or more feet high, its corners and edges smoothed as if wave swept. This was a curiosity in that land, where there were few stones or rocks of any kind. Having studied our "Child's Book of Knowledge", we decided it must be a meteorite. We sometimes rode or drove over to it, had picnics in its shadow, and tried to climb the polished sides. It was actually, as an expert explained to us later, a glacial rock, possibly carried thousands of miles, and deposited there when the ice age of centuries ago was melting, and pushing its glaciers over the continent.

J.Key

Mary Ann Bottomley

For all sad words of tongue or pen
The saddest are these "It might have been."

John Greenleaf Whittier - Maud Muller

Pretty, gentle, Mary Ann Bottomley, died very suddenly on July 29th, 1910, only a few weeks after we reached Radfords. She had worked very hard assisting Mother during those first difficult days, moving heavy furniture about, carrying things up and down stairs, and she must have suffered a great deal from the heat. Nobody knew she had a weak heart, and she never complained. She was often breathless, and sometimes sat down suddenly to rest for a minute, but no one dreamed there was anything seriously wrong with her. One morning she fainted, and collapsed on the floor. Father drove into Strathmore to fetch the doctor, was fortunate to find him in town, and brought him out as quickly as possible, but Boppo died just as they arrived.

Mary Ann Bottomley's death made a terrific impact on me - it was my first experience with death and suddenly it dawned on me that life was not a permanent thing, that people like flowers and weeds might fade and wither away, and were gone forever. It was hard to believe that Boppo, who that morning had talked and laughed, and eaten breakfast with us, was not there anymore, would never talk to us again. At the time I do not think I felt any real grief, nor great sense of loss, just an enormous curiosity.

After the doctor left, on the day Boppo died, the body was laid on the bed in her room, the door shut, and Mother warned us that nobody was to go in. Late that night when all was quiet and the house dark, I slipped out of bed and crept across the passage to Boppo's door. I stood for minutes with my hand on the doorknob, shivering in the hot darkness, then slowly turned it, making no sound, pushed the door open and slipped inside. On the bedside table, a lamp turned low, shed a pool of light across the white spread that was pulled up over the bed. The window blind was down, and except for the dim light by the bed, the room was in darkness. I could see Boppo's form under the spread. Holding my breath I tiptoed over to the bed, and put out my hand towards the corner of the coverlet, intending to pull it back and look at Boppo's face, but something held me back. I couldn't do it! It seemed as if a silent "No!" froze my hand. After a minute I crept quickly out again, closing the door silently, and crossed the dark passage to the room I shared with Betty. She was still sound asleep as I slipped into bed, but I lay awake for a long time staring into the darkness.

At that time there was no undertaker nearer than Calgary, and in the hot weather it was very necessary to bury the dead within a day or two. With the help of a neighbour Father made a coffin out of rough lumber, and a grave was dug in the southwest corner of the farm on the top of a little rise.

The news of the death and funeral, had spread over the countryside. Early in the morning, of the day of the funeral, buggies, wagons, and riders on horseback, appeared on the prairie trails heading towards Radfords, and soon men, women, and children filled the farmyard. They unpacked picnic lunches, and much to Mother's consternation, the women took over the kitchen, filled the copper washboiler with water, heated it to boiling on the range, and made coffee for everybody. Farmers, ranchers, and their wives, sat about the yard in any shade they could find, chatting and visiting with each other, and the children played happily in the barns and corrals. It was more like a community picnic than a funeral.

In the early afternoon, the Rev. T.W. Castle, at that time Rector of St. Michael and All Angels in Strathmore, arrived, greeted everybody, and then went into the house to change into his vestments. In a few minutes he came out again, looking impressive in his cassock and surplice. Then the coffin was brought out of the house, and carried through the pasture to the grave site. The crowd, now quiet, followed behind, and stepped carefully over the gopher holes and round badger diggings. Mother ducks with flotillas of half grown ducklings sailed busily about the weedy slough below the house, and meadowlarks trilled their cheerful summer song from the rosebushes and clumps of buckbrush. A gentle breeze tempered the heat of the sun.

Mother had made a wreath from wild flowers, roses, paintbrush, gaillardias and black eyed susans, intertwined with the silvery grey of the little velvety plant we called prairie lavender, because it had an aromatic fragrance. This had been placed on top of the coffin.

Mr. Castle read the burial service, the coffin was lowered into the grave, and earth shovelled in. The closing prayers were read, and then the congregation drifted slowly back to the house. Goodbyes were said, and gradually the buggies and wagons pulled away across the prairie in the late afternoon sunshine.

Later on, a fence was built round the grave, and years later, when Radfords was sold, Father had the coffin exhumed and reburied, in St, Michael and All Angels' cemetery in Strathmore.

One day during the following fall, a buggy and horse from the Strathmore livery stable pulled up to the farm gate, and a young man jumped out, tied his horse to a fencepost and walked up the drive. He met Father coming up from the barn, and they stood talking for a minute. Then Father laid his hand on his shoulder, and took him into the house. Sometime later they came out again, and Mother was now with them. They walked slowly down to the gate, and I looked curiously at the visitor, as they passed where we were playing near the driveway. He was tall and good looking, and as I look back to that day,

I can remember the expression on his face, a still tautness, as he walked stiffly between our parents, looking straight in front of him. They shook hands, and Father put his hand on his arm as he stepped into the buggy. The young man gathered up the reins, turned the horse around, and drove off along the trail towards Strathmore.

Mother told us some time later who he was, and what had brought him out to Radfords. He and Boppo had been secretly engaged, before they had both left England, he to emigrate to the United States to find work, and she to Canada with us. When letters suddenly stopped, he was naturally concerned, and as soon as he could raise sufficient money, and leave work, he had come up to find out what had happened. Mother and Father had the sad responsibility of breaking the news to him, of the tragic death of his fiancee. They had known nothing of the secret engagement.

I never knew his name, and as far as I can remember we never heard of him again.

Christmas 1910

AT RADFORDS, STRATHMORE

At Christmas play and make good cheer
For Christmas comes but once a year.

From the Farmer's Daily Diet

That was a strange Christmas - our first Christmas at the new Radfords. No Christmas tree, no holly nor ivy, no fragrant cedar boughs entwined around the walls. In fact there was not a green thing to be seen anywhere, in that vast expanse of frozen white wilderness.

Early in December we had our first blizzard. The day before, as the afternoon waned, ominous sundogs had appeared on each side of the sun, clouds, like bundles of dirty fleece, scudded across the sky from the north, and drove low over the land, thicker and thicker, until they melded and blotted out the sky. The wind had strengthened, bringing the first flakes of white. Soon the air was full of driving snow, fine and hard as salt. Sky and land disappeared, and we seemed to be suspended in a fantasy world of whirling white.

The temperature dropped, and it was hard to keep the house warm even with the cookstove and heaters going day and night. We had a cellar full of coal and wood, as that fall, Father and a neighbour, with three tiered wagons and four horse teams had driven forty miles to Carbon, on the Red Deer River, and brought back loads of coal. A supply of poplar wood had been brought from the Bow Valley. Frost formed thickly on all the windows, and we heated pennies on the stove and pressed them into the frost so that we could peer out at the great banks of snow. The blizzard swept over us for three days, and then the wind dropped, the sky cleared and a dazzling sun shone on the hard packed drifts. Our animals had been safely housed in the stable and cowshed, and with the help of our one hired man, Father managed to shovel a path down to the barnyard, to feed and water them every day.

Christmas Eve, we were all in the warm kitchen. We had had supper, the big black iron cookstove crackled and sent out blasts of heat, and a kettle on the back was singing comfortably. The twins were already tucked into their cots, and Betty, Tommy and I were playing quietly. Mother and Father were sitting in front of the stove with the oven door open, reading months old newspapers which had come out from England. Large parcels from Grandmother Petter, Grandfather Pardon, and various aunts, had arrived earlier, with plum puddings, cakes, shortbread and sweets, and Christmas presents, still unopened, for all of us.

But it did not feel like Christmas Eve. I think I was old enough to realize a little of all that was missing, family gatherings, friends, parties, and to feel something of the loneliness and homesickness of our parents.

Suddenly we heard what was at that time a very strange sound, voices, far off singing. In 1910, of course, there was no radio, no television, and we had no gramophone, no possible way that music could be transmitted into our home from the outside. I remember looking up at father, thinking he was playing some kind of practical joke on us, but he was looking as startled as the rest of us. Ted, the hired man, jumped up, ran to the back door, pulled it open, and pushed back the heavy storm door. We all clustered round him and stared out into the moonlit night. There, in the deep snow, stood half a dozen bundled up forms, and they were singing carols! Suddenly there was shouting and laughter, and the kitchen was full of people. They peeled off their snowy coats and gathered around the hot stove, rubbing their cold hands. They were the sons and daughters or our neighbours, the Worthingtons and Mercers, and they had struggled through the miles of snowdrifts between our farms to bring us Christmas greetings. It was a marvellously exciting and heart warming event. Mother and Ted soon had cups of hot tea, Christmas cake, mince tarts, and shortbread laid out on the table.

Now the air was full of Christmas spirit, the magic, excitement and happiness of Christmasses past. Mother was smiling, Father chatting enthusiastically, as he passed round the mince tarts.

The happy young visitors stayed for a couple of hours, and then bundled up again in their mackinaws, overshoes, scarves, and woollen caps, started out into the frosty night for their homes. We were soon tucked into our beds, stockings were hung on the brass bed rails, and we drifted off to sleep, reassured that Father Christmas remembered us - would find us- and that all was well.

A winter sleigh ride.
Buffalo horns decorate
the house.

In Wintertime

You may have tangible wealth untold;
Caskets of jewels and coffers of gold.
Richer than I you can never be -
I had a Mother who read to me.

From The Reading Mother
by Strickland Gillilan

During those first winters at the new
Radfords, when we were often shut in the house
for days on end, and the howling blizzards, deep
drifts of snow, and the bitter cold isolated us
from our neighbours, Mother read to us in the
long winter evenings.

Sitting in the kitchen, with the big iron
cookstove crackling, and glowing with the red hot
coal, and the oven door open,to throw out the
heat, Mother would read by the light of a coal
oil lamp. Early in the evening, before the
younger children went to bed, we had fairy
stories, Grimm's of course, and some from two
large, well illustrated books of fairy tales,
translated from Russian and Norwegian , such
beautiful and fascinating stories, that those
countries are still lands of fantasy to me.

Mother read beautifully. She was something of
an actress, and as she read the characters came
alive, and she made the dialogue so realistic,
changing her voice to suit each character and
situation. In the flickering lamplight, and with
the dark background closing around us, we lived
in storyland. And sometimes Mother recited poems
to us - John Gilpin, Widdicombe Fair, and the
Jackdaw of Rheims, and in time we knew them all
by heart, and would sometimes join in, especially
with the choruses such as, "Old Uncle Tom
Cobleigh and a' and a', Old Uncle Tom Cobleigh
and a'!"

As we grew older,she read to us such classics

as, Dicken's- A Christmas Carol,The Old Curiosity
Shop, David Copperfield, and Harrison Ainsworth's
Old St. Paul's and the Tower of London. Our
favourite was Lorna Doone. Mother in her younger
years had ridden and walked with her brothers and
sisters over Exmoor, and had explored the gloomy,
mysterious Doone Valley; had even seen Jan Ridd's
name carved on the desk in the old school house
on the Moor, which he had attended. Eden Phill-
potts was a distant relative of the Pardon
family, and Mother read to us The Farm of the
Dagger, and his Devonshire Village Tales, so full
of folklore, and Mother would imitate the soft,
drawled Devonshire dialect.

Mother's father, John Pardon, and his brother
Arthur had inherited a publishing and printing
business,in Paternoster Row in London, from their
father Benjamin, and although then retired, our
Grandfather was still very interested in the
publishing business, and sent us many parcels of
good books, carefully wrapped in heavy brown
paper, and well tied with string. Before long I
was reading everything I could lay my hands on.
Robinson Crusoe, Swiss Family Robinson, Uncle
Tom's Cabin, - a fascinating introduction to
American history. Then Louise M. Alcott's Little
Women, Laddie and Freckles by Gene Stratton
Porter, The Dog Crusoe by Ballantyne, and many
more stories of our New World.

Our parents were very long suffering,
realizing how boring it was for us to be shut in
the house for days, and sometimes weeks at a
time. We invented games, often boisterous and
quarrelsome, sometimes piling the heavy leather
seated diningroom chairs into pyramids and then
climbing to the top, with of course occasional
disastrous results. In the evenings we played
dominoes, tiddley-winks, snap and Happy Family.

During those gloomy winter months three cats
contributed a good deal to our indoor amusement.
Twinky, a silvery grey and white tom, belonged to
Betty. Mine was a large brown and gold tabby,
Widdy, and Barbara owned a rather cranky little

female, white with large brown and black spots
all over her, and of course she was named Spotty.
We loved them and played with them, but they had
an amazing way, when they had had enough of our
games, of disappearing. They were supposed to
sleep in the cellar at night, but when our
bedtime drew near they would be nowhere to be
found. Twinky would have crawled under somebody's
feather comforter on one of the beds. Widdy and
Spotty would be curled up in some dark corner
well out of sight, then when all were asleep, the
house silent, and the lamps out, they would creep
out and spend the night tucked in beside us,
their soft warm bodies more comforting than any
teddy bear.

An hour or so most mornings would be taken up
with our "lessons" under Miss Gwen Southwell's
supervision,(when she could spare the time from
household chores),doing sums, writing laborious
copperplate exercises with pen and ink, light
strokes up, dark strokes down,or studying Little
Arthur's English History. As we grew older, we
began helping with the housework, churning the
butter, washing the cream separator, sweeping
the floor with a stiff corn broom. Then as the
winter waned, and the spring work began, we would
be out rounding up the milk cows, and feeding the
pigs and chickens.

Childhood was short for the children of the
prairie pioneers. Boys of ten and twelve worked
in the fields, driving four and six horse teams
on the ploughs and binders, sowing the crops,
raking in the haying season, and stooking, come
harvest time. Of necessity, we had to take on
many responsibilities, and life soon became a
serious business. Yes, we grew up quickly on the
farms in those days.

Roy Frith, Aunt Mary's brother-in-law, stayed
with us for a year or two, helping Father and
learning prairie farming. One gloomy fall day he
came back from Strathmore with a large packing
case and a big black thing under his arm, a horn,
something like the ear trumpets that the deaf

depended on in those days, but much larger. He
unpacked the case and set a square black box on a
table. Then he studied a sheet of instructions,
on which was a picture of a white fox terrier
sitting in front of the trumpet, head on one side
in a listening attitude, and with the printed
words, "His Master's Voice", curling out of the
mouth of the trumpet. Roy attached the horn to
the black box, then with much fiddling and
adjusting, inserted a black tube into its side.
By this time, of course, the entire family and
Gwen Southwell were standing around watching,
asking questions and making comments. Then Roy
screwed a metal handle into the back of the black
box and twiddled it round and round. Some squeaks
and grating noises came from the mouth of the
trumpet, and to our amazement a man's voice could
be heard. Then suddenly the room was filled with
music! It was rather harsh and strident, but
recognizable as a well known dance tune.

Roy rolled up the sheepskin rugs, grabbed
Gwen by the arm and then they were waltzing round
and round on the oilcloth floor; the children
were hopping and skipping about; Mother was
clapping her hands, and Father sat on a chair in
a corner, laughing and rolling himself a
cigarette.

This, of course, was Edison's Phonograph, one
of the first to be seen in the district, a great
innovation. Up until then we had no musical
instrument, other than the great black piano on
which Gwen was to give us lessons, but it had not
been tuned since it left Yeovil, and while Gwen
could play it, she declared it was so terribly
out of tune, she would not touch it again until
it was tuned. As there was no piano tuner
available nearer than Calgary at that time, the
piano remained shut and silent. With no radio or
television in the homes in those days, music of
any kind was a great treat and excitement.

Christmas Concert

NIGHTINGALE SCHOOL   1911

"Heap on more wood -
The wind is chill
But let it whistle all it will
We'll keep our Christmas merry still.

Sir Walter Scott - Christmas in Olden Time

The stars glittered in the enormous black velvet dome of the sky, and the moon, high and remote, was like a tiny brilliant silver disk, its perimeter clear cut against the shimmering backdrop. It was very cold, but still, and the horses' breath plumed out in misty gusts, as they trotted along the hard frozen snow packed road. The hayrack on runners, glided smoothly and easily along. Father had it half filled with hay, and well wrapped up in our heavy coats, with tasseled woollen toques on our heads, and feet in buckled overshoes, we burrowed down into it for warmth. The grown ups, Mother and Father, Roy and Gwen, sat on the hay with horse blankets over their knees.

The little one room schoolhouse was well filled when we arrived, men, women, and children, young and old, all gay and excited. Festoons of coloured paper were hung across the ceiling, and big red and green crinkled paper bells hung here and there. Near the door, a large red hot heater sent out lovely blasts of warmth, as shovelsful of coal were thrown in.

We were not pupils of the school, as we were still being given "lessons" at home. However, the friendly young school teacher had driven down to Radfords some time ahead of the Christmas Concert, to give us all special invitations. She suggested to Mother that we children, Betty, Tommy, the twins and myself, might like to take part in the concert. The twins, then about three and a half, had learned a little poem, and

Mother, pleased at the thought, said they would recite it together.

A small temporary stage had been set up at one end of the schoolroom, and grey blankets strung on a wire served as a curtain. Soon after we arrived, the teacher walked out onto the stage, and announced that the programme would start with all singing Oh Canada, and then the pupils would sing some choruses. The Maple Leaf Forever, Jingle Bells, Au Clair de la Lune and other well known Canadian songs were sung with gusto and vociferously applauded. Although at that time we knew neither the words nor the tunes of these songs, Betty, Tommy and I, had been invited to stand up with the class. I remember feeling very foolish standing there, a head taller than the others, and unable to sing a note. After a while, I started opening and shutting my mouth, and trying to twist my face into appropriate expressions, in an attempt to appear that I was actually singing. At least I was in the back row, but poor Betty and Tommy were in the front, and had to stand there, silent and bewildered, through the whole thing.

Somebody recited a long poem, then came the twin's turn. They stood side by side, shoulder touching shoulder for moral support, in the middle of the little stage. They were dressed in beautifully smocked wool flannel dresses, one in pale blue and one in pale pink, with short white socks and black kid slippers. Their chubby knees were pink and dimpled, and each head was a halo of pale gold curls. Sissie was always the leader of the two. Gentle little Laetitia so often tagged along after her, chirping "Me too!" "Me too!" that Father nicknamed her "Me Too", and she was called this all through her childhood years.

Mother stood just out of sight behind the curtain, and we heard her prompt them. Then swaying gently from side to side to the rhythm, they got off to a good start;

"A little grey squirrel lived up in a tree,
As happy a squirrel as ever could be.

With nuts for his dinner and nuts for his tea
That little grey squirrel that lived in a
tree."

They recited the last line without a hitch,
and now were supposed to bow, but here something
went awry. Instead of coming to a finish, they
hesitated, not quite sure where they were, then
continued with the second line, "As happy a
squirrel as ever could be", and proceeded to
repeat the poem to the end, again the
hesitation, then cheerfully off again for the
third time to the end. By this time the audience
was becoming aware of what was happening, and
chuckles of amusement could be heard here and
there. In a minute the whole room was shouting
with laughter. The twins drowned out, came to a
slow stop. But, they reacted differently to the
applause and laughter. Sissie was laughing
gleefully with the audience, but little Me Too's
large blue eyes filled with tears, and in a
moment they were cascading down her chubby
cheeks. Mother ran in from the side, and gathered
them up, one under each arm, and carried them off
the stage.

When the concert was over Santa Claus, Father
Christmas to us, arrived with much shouting and
laughter and excitement. He bounced out onto the
stage in his red tunic, with bushy beard and wig
made out of sheep's wool. There was no Christmas
tree, but a large galvanized washtub, piled high
with gifts was dragged out from behind the
curtain, and each child was called up in turn, to
receive a white tissue paper wrapped present, and
a little green net bag of jelly beans. After this
was over, steaming fragrant coffee, plates piled
with large thick sandwiches, and cakes of all
kinds were handed around.

One difficult problem mothers had to face
with winter gatherings such as this Christmas
party, was the toilet arrangements for the babies
and small children. Obviously they could not all
be bundled up, and taken out into the bitter cold
and deep snow, to the little outdoor privies

every time they needed to go. Our Mother solved
the matter for the twins by making a drawstring
bag out of dark green felt, into which she tucked
a small grey enamel chamberpot, and this was
taken with us to such events as the concert. This
was used by the younger children in one of the
cloakrooms, and then somebody carried it out a
convenient back door, and emptied it into a
snowdrift. Father said this invention of Mother's
should be patented!

On this particular occasion, after the
refreshments had been served, there was to be a
dance. The fiddles were tuning up, it was time
for us to go, and we were bundled into our coats
and overshoes. Father and Roy went out to hitch
up the team, which in common with the other
horses, had been tied, covered with horse
blankets, to the fence posts around the
schoolyard.

The cloakrooms were at the end of the
schoolroom farthest from the main door. By the
time we were ready to leave, the floor was
already filled with hop-scotching dancers, so we
had to squeeze our way down the side of the room
to the door. It was my responsibility to carry
the green felt bag, and being half asleep, full
of ham sandwiches, and quite bemused by the
dancing feet and merry fiddling, I lagged behind
the others. About half way down the hall,
unfortunately, I held the bag upside down.
Suddenly the little enamel pot bounced out onto
the floor, a passing foot caught it, and it went
clattering into the middle of the dancers.
Horrified, I dived in between the legs trying to
catch it, but by then the happy crowd had
recognized it, and it was being joyfully kicked
here and there. I gave up, and stood red faced in
the middle of the floor, until somebody kindly
took pity on me, picked up the little pot by its
handle, and tucked it back into the bag, which
was hanging from my hand. I was then hustled out
of the door to catch up with the rest of the
family, thankful that they had not seen my

shattering experience. I never mentioned it to anybody, and although Mother and Father no doubt heard about it in days to come, and probably had a good laugh, it was never referred to in my hearing. I was not teased, and my bruised ego soon recovered.

As I look back upon that particular event, I recall that as children we called the chamberpot, an item which in those days was to be found in every bedroom and nursery, a "ha ha". We had learned this from the nursemaid who had lived with us and cared for us, from the time I was born, until we left for Canada. Looking up the term in the Oxford Dictionary, I find "ha ha" defined as a "sunk fence, bounding park or garden." No doubt, in earlier days before such luxuries as running water, and indoor bathrooms, and flush toilets, it would be customary, and quite acceptable, to retire when necessary, to the bottom of the garden to the ha ha, a "sunk fence" or ditch, which would also be a form of sewer into which household slops would be emptied.

Interesting theory?

Akenstad School 1912

"Three little maids from school are we
Pert as a schoolgirl well can be
Filled to the brim with girlish glee!"

The Mikado

When Tommy was about six, Betty eight, and I ten years old, we went to a little one room prairie school called Akenstad, about two or three miles from our farm.

There was a Dutch colony near Akenstad, and there were one or two Belgian families farming in the area, so that most of the pupils were Dutch or Belgian. They spoke broken but understandable English, and I had a special friend, in a Dutch girl, about my age, Johanna. She was large and mature for her age, with long brown hair braided in thick plaits, gentle brown eyes, and plump pink cheeks. We had long discussions during the recesses, wandering about on the prairie, picking crocuses, or gaillardias.

We took our lunches in lard pails, large meat or jam sandwiches, raisin scones thickly buttered, and sometimes even an orange or apple, and when the weather was warm, and the mosquitoes not too voracious, we would sit outside on the schoolhouse steps and make a picnic out of it. A large bucket of cold water with a tin dipper stood by the school door, and we all drank the water out of the same dipper.

The Akenstad teacher at that time came from Ontario, and her geography lessons were mainly about Canada. She told us fascinating stories about the Canadian Arctic, polar bears, Eskimos, timber wolves, and seals, and the early exploration of the West. For homework she would have us study our geography books, and draw maps of Canada. She was a cheerful, good looking young woman, her dark brown hair swept up off her forehead and rolled up at the back. She usually wore a navy blue dress of alpaca, buttoned down the front and fitted tightly over her shapely and firmly moulded figure. She boarded with a Dutch family, and one warm Sunday in spring Mother invited her to have tea with us. Father drove up to fetch her, and when she stepped down out of the buggy, I gazed entranced at her beautiful dress of white muslin, the full skirt flowing down over her slim ankles, and a wide blue satin sash tied round her tiny waist. I made up my mind then and there that I would have a dress like that someday.

We drove ourselves to school in a two wheeled trap, or dog cart as we called it, pulled by a large, elderly black horse named Lucy. She considered herself retired, and seldom would consent to trot. We were driving home one afternoon, on what was then the open prairie. The trail wound over a low hill, past a large, deep gravel pit. Just as we were passing it, a white dog suddenly jumped over the edge of the pit, almost under Lucy's nose. She leaped into the air, took the bit in her teeth, and raced off down the slope, and round the edge of a slough towards home. The high wheeled, light weight buggy bumped and bounced from one wheel to the other, over the gopher and badger holes. Betty and I managed to hang on to the seat, but Tommy slid to the floor, clutched the dashboard with both hands, and softly wailed over and over again;

"We'll be dead in a minute! We'll be dead in a minute!"

However, poor old Lucy soon ran out of breath, slowed down as we rounded the farm corner post, and we arrived home safely, none the worse.

AKENSTAD SCHOOL - 1912

Edith Petter, the author's mother out for a drive in a governess cart, or trap. In Canada the Petter children had a similar trap to drive to school.

Picnic at Bow River

A picnic! Good idea, a day off from the never ending work on the farm. A drive across the spring green, flower sprinkled prairie to some pleasant spot, near a creek perhaps, where we would find some shade under the fragrant wolf-willow, and newly leafed poplars. Mother and Father were discussing this after a late supper, and Betty and I were listening, eyes sparkling, nudging each other excitedly. Yes, a good idea!

"There's plenty of bread for sandwiches - and the rest of the potted veal - I'll make a dried apple tart -" Mother was thinking out loud. "Betty and Joan can come, the younger children had better stay home with Dorothy, they wouldn't enjoy a long drive." The daughter of a neighbouring farmer was staying with us at that time, helping with the housework.

It was 1912. The rush of the heavy spring work, ploughing, discing, seeding, and harrowing, had lessened, the crops were in, haying had not yet started, there was a brief lull. It was a good time to take a day's holiday. Father had wanted for some time to show Mother the Bow River which wound its way across the prairie a few miles south of Strathmore. It would be a long drive, but we would start early, and take the democrat with Kitty and Maud, who were strong and fresh and trotted well. Of course, the mosquitoes and flies would be troublesome, but so they were wherever we happened to be, and we had the bottles of strong smelling repellant to rub over our arms and legs.

In Yeovil, England, in the drowsy, leisurely summer days, family picnics out in the sun filled meadows of the countryside were among the happiest of occasions. Before the days of the motor car, a hayrack or wagon, with driver and team of strong cart horses would be hired for the day. Large wicker hampers would be filled with food, cold roasts of beef, ham, loaves of crusty

73

bread to be sliced and spread thickly with
butter, which would be packed into a wooden bowl.
There would be a couple of dozen or more of hard
boiled eggs, a large solid fruit cake, yellow
with saffron, strawberries and raspberries with
thick, clotted Devonshire cream, or apples, pears
and plums, depending on the season, and cans of
cold tea, with milk for the children, all of
which would make a handsome meal.

Grandparents, Uncles, and Aunts, and cousins,
would be picked up at the various homes, and
would be driven out along the shady hedge lined
lanes to Ham Hill, or Nine Springs. They would
spend long happy hours in the quiet fields, the
older members drowsing and chatting, on the soft
green turf, in the shade of the lofty beeches and
elms. Others would climb the rolling hills, watch
the rabbits gamboling in their warrens, or play
hide and seek in the shady woods.

Then would come the big event of the outing.
A white linen cloth would be spread on the grass
and the food laid out. China plates, cups and
saucers, knives and forks, salt and pepper, and
of course, linen serviettes, would be formally
arranged. Then the family would seat themselves
in a merry ring. Later the wagon would return,
and the picnickers would climb in and drive home
in the peaceful, golden evening, tired and well
fed, the sunlight slanting low through the trees,
and the blackbirds chirping happily in the
branches.

Now, in Alberta, a different kind of picnic
was being planned. We had a man working steadily
for us at the time, a reliable farm hand who
would look after the milking and feeding of the
animals while we were away, so Father felt he
could safely take the day off.

We were up bright and early that warm, clear
spring day. The food had been packed the night
before, and as soon as we had finished breakfast
the horses were hitched to the democrat, which
had two comfortable double seats and spare space
at the back for the picnic hamper. Mother and

Father sat in the front seat, Betty and I in the back. We drove along the road allowance for a couple of miles, then the wagon trail wound up the long slow incline, to the top of the rise, where we could look out over the great flat expanse of mostly unfenced range land to the south and east. Father pulled the horses to a stop, they needed a rest and the sun was getting warmer. Mother put up her sunshade and Father pushed his wide straw hat off his forehead. He pointed to a little huddle of buildings in the distance.

"That's Gleichen" he said, "And right over there on the horizon, if you look hard enough, you might see Brooks."

He cupped his hands over his eyes and peered out over the prairie. We could see the line of the railway, which at that time was the main line of the C.P.R. Below us and about a mile away was a small, round slough, now full with the spring rains, and reflecting as clearly as a mirror the brilliant blue of the sky. A herd of range cattle surrounded it. They were Herefords, we could see the white faces and long curved horns. Some were standing in the shallow water and others lying on the turf, chewing their cud and taking their morning rest.

A few miles south of Strathmore the Bow River, flowing deep between its coulee serrated cutbanks, loops up in a great curve northwards, and we now followed the trail which led towards the top of the curve. The sun was warm, but the air was fresh and invigorating, as the horses trotted steadily along. Sometime in the late morning we reached the cutbanks, and looked down over the river flats spread out below. Clumps of trees, poplar, birch and willow, and here and there the darker spike of a conifer, lined the river itself, a lovely setting for our picnic. The trail we had been following led down the sloping side of a coulee, and we drove down to the grassy flats. We unhitched the horses and led them down to the river to drink, then tethered them to a tree and gave each a bag of oats. They needed nourishment, and a good rest before we started the long drive homewards.

After the picnic lunch we explored the riverbank, watching the churning water, still in its spring spate, swirling high between its sandy banks. Then Betty and I decided we would climb up one of the coulees, where a cow or sheep path led up through the scrub. Near the top was a flat stretch of about an acre, still below the level of the flat prairie, with a few spindly poplars and scrubby underbrush. There were some rough wooden crosses standing here and there, leaning this way and that, the wood old and weathered, and as we crept curiously about, we saw still older ones lying in the undergrowth, disintegrating into the soil.

"It's a graveyard!" I whispered, "Some people are buried here."

Near the centre was a little oblong enclosure, surrounded by a fence of wooden slats, the wood newer than the crosses, and we tiptoed towards this, and gazed down over the fence at the little grave. Lying on the grass we were astonished to see a child's wooden toy, a little truck with wooden wheels, and a string of brightly coloured glass beads arranged in a circle.

We stood silently, staring at these things, and no doubt were planning to climb over the fence and examine them, when something made me look over my shoulder. A horse was standing just behind us, with a tall Indian sitting on it, bareback, horse and rider absolutely motionless. They were not more than a couple of yards from us but we had not heard a sound. The Indian was looking down at us, his face quite expressionless and his dark eyes, over the fine aquiline nose, watched us without a flicker, the firm, straight mouth so motionless he might have been a carved statue. It would have been hard to tell whether he was laughing at us, or preparing to scalp us.

The picture he made is so clear in my memory,

the tall, proud, straight figure, the reddish brown skin, and dark hair pulled smoothly back into a ponytail. He was probably a Cree or Stoney, of the true Red Indian breed of the plains. He was well dressed in fringed buckskins and brown shirt. His feet, in beaded moccasins, hung well down below his horse's belly.

Betty must have seen him at the same moment, as she clutched my arm frantically, and with eyes fixed on the still motionless figure, we sidled round the little grave, then raced through the tangled grass towards the cutbank that curved smoothly downwards. Panting, we stumbled and fell and rolled, scrambled up, fell again, and rolled to the bottom. When we reached the rest of the family we gasped out our story, so thankful that we had escaped to safety. Father stood up.

"We must be on a reserve! Maybe I'd better see if he is still up there, and explain we are just here to see the Bow, and don't intend to intrude on them."

Mother looked rather worried and started gathering up the remains of the picnic and the rugs. Father climbed the cutbank, and we anxiously watched him disappear into the scrubby bush at the top of the coulee. After a while he came back tramping assuredly down the trail, saying that he could see no Indian anywhere. Perhaps we had imagined it all?

Betty and I, who were examining our torn stockings and scraped knees, declared indignantly that we had certainly seen the Indian, it had been no fairy story. We hadn't made it up! Father listened quietly to us, then turned and glancing up the coulee and along the river flats, hurried over to the horses, and hitched them to the democrat. The family was soon packed in, and we started on the long drive back to Radfords.

A gentle breeze from the west, cool and refreshing, met us as we topped the cutbanks. The sun was now gliding towards the west, and a golden heat haze had spread along the horizon. The tired horses plodded slowly along the trail, their heads down and ears forward as we neared the farm.

Betty and I were not the only ones to have something to talk about on the way home. Mother had found the nest of a teal duck, still with the newly hatched ducklings, balls of tawny fluff, in it. The distraught mother duck had flopped and flapped about in the long grass, and dropped a brilliant blue feather, which Mother tucked into the hatband of her big straw hat. Father was sure he had seen a rainbow trout in the Bow, and speculated about returning someday with fishing gear, if the area were not an Indian Reserve. In spite of Betty's and my frightening encounter, it had been a lovely, happy day, a day to remember.

Father learned later, that sometime in the latter half of the eighteenth century, there had been a Roman Catholic mission to the Indian tribes in that part of Alberta, and the foundations and crumbled remains of an old log building, believed to be the Church mission, had been found in the bush on the banks of the Bow River. The cemetery Betty and I had explored, was probably part of the Mission, and was still used from time to time by the Indians.

Gypsies and Indians

During the autumn before we left England,
when I was six, Father had taken me to a fair on
the outskirts of Yeovil. There had been many
gypsies wandering about among the crowd, and I
had been a little afraid of them, but fascinated
by the dark, bold faces and flashing eyes. I had
had a wonderful time riding the horses on the
merry-go-round and a sort of ferris wheel had
whirled us up into the starry sky.

As we walked home that evening, we had passed
Grandmother's house and although it was quite
dark, and must have been long past my bedtime, we
went in. She was sitting bolt upright in her
drawingroom, her stiff black silk dress spread
out around her, a beautifully pleated white
muslin cap on her grey hair, and a large gold
watch hung on a long chain, was tucked into her
waistband. I don't suppose she was yet sixty, but
to me she was an old, old lady. There were what
my Father called "ructions", with sundry uncles
and aunts joining in the discussion, as
Grandmother did not approve of anything as
frivolous as a fair for young or old. I clutched
my bag of sweet, gingery brandy snaps, and
listened with flattered interest, as the grownups
argued over my head about the foolhardiness, if
not actual wickedness, of exposing a child of my
tender years to such sinfulness, not to mention
all the "things" that I might pick up.

In the early days of this century, small
bands of the true gypsies roamed across the
United States from coast to coast, and at times,
up into Southern Canada. Sometime during the
first year of two after we arrived at Radfords, a
small band of what were thought to be Indians,
camped on the unfenced, bald prairie about a mile
north of us. Mother was certain that these were
not Indians, but gypsies. They were swarthy,
their features finer than the red Indians, and
unlike the Indians, both men and women wore

brightly coloured scarves tied over their heads. They travelled in wagons and democrats, and as far as I remember they had little to do with any of the settlers in the district. They were there only for a day or two and then mysteriously disappeared.

Also at this time small bands of Indians wandered about the prairie, camping in tepees and tents, on the outskirts of towns and ranches. They were Crees and Stonies, Blackfeet and Bloods, the true Red Indians of the Western Plains, the men tall and proud with aquiline features, and the women good looking, at least in their younger years, but they were aloof and had little to do with the white settlers. Mother was a little afraid of the Indians and likened them to the gypsies that had roamed the lanes and byways of Britain in their caravans, thieving and begging.

Shortly after we had arrived at Strathmore, Mother and Mary Ann Bottomley had been in the kitchen one day, when something had made Mother turn around, to find two tall Indian men standing close behind them. They had opened the door and walked in without making a sound. After staring at the speechless women for a moment, they calmly turned round and walked out, without a word spoken, leaving the door open. Understandably, Mother felt that Indians and Gypsies were probably alike and not to be trusted.

Now, we heard that many of these Indians from all over Alberta were gathering at Calgary for this thing called a stampede.

Calgary Stampede 1912

"The origin and development of the Calgary Stampede is steeped in history. Back in 1912 a rangy cowpuncher from the State of Wyoming named Guy Weadick, came to Calgary and after a time managed to interest four big cattlemen in financing a venture, which was planned as the greatest Frontier Day's Show or Roundup ever held in North America. He called it "The Stampede". The prize was $40,000 in gold, and cowboys from all over Canada, the United States and Mexico answered the call.

The show was held at the Exhibition Grounds, in September 1912. It was opened by the Duke of Connaught, son of Queen Victoria of England, and the then Governor General of Canada."

Quoted from "A Short History of the Calgary Exhibition and Stampede."

Author Unknown

We were up early that fine September morning, and were eating breakfast in the fresh, cool kitchen when the golden sun topped the horizon, and sent long level rays across the prairie to gild the distant mountain peaks in the west. There was a hint of fall in the air, but it was going to be a hot day, one of those glorious days in early fall, when summer returns to take one last glowing fling, before gathering her skirts for her final departure. The sky was the colour of skim milk, just faintly blue, not a cloud marred its silken dome, and already heat waves were shimmering in the distance, confusing the horizon, so that the flat expanse of the prairie merged into the pale sky.

"Your mother wouldn't approve of your taking her to the fair, you know." Mother was dishing up the porridge at the great black cookstove, Father smiled at me and I held my breath, could Mother change her mind? I had known Mother had not wanted me to go to Calgary with Father, but he had promised to take me.

"But, my dear, it isn't exactly a fair." Father said. "It's called a stampede. Quite a different kettle of fish. Most educational, and besides it is going to be opened by the Duke of Connaught!" Mother was not impressed.

"Well, I hope she doesn't pick up something. Keep her out of the way of those gypsies." I breathed again and started on my porridge.

Father had hitched the horses to the wagon before breakfast, and they were tied outside the kitchen door in readiness for our early start. Mother tied on my sunbonnet. My sisters and I all wore sunbonnets then. Mother made them for us out of bright cotton print, the large stitched brims that flared out around our faces stiffened with starch. They were tied under our chins with ribbons, and there were flaps of print at the back to keep the sun off our necks.

Father carried out the parcel of sandwiches, and a bottle of cold, sweet tea, and stowed them in the wagon. It was still very early, my sisters and Dorothy Evans, who was Mothers's help at that time, were still asleep, but Mother came out to see us off. We climbed into the wagon and Father gathered up the reins, waved his big straw hat, cracked the whip, and the horses broke into a trot. We were off on one of those joyous outings that are the highlights of my memories of those days, the jaunts that my Father and I took together. There was a close bond between us, just to be with him was pure happiness, and besides, any expedition of Father's had an exciting tendency toward the unexpected.

The seat was a wide board, hung on springs to the sides of the wagonbox, and we jounced and bounced along as the wagon jolted over the trail. Gophers, curious and unafraid, sat on top of their sandy mounds, and stood bolt upright to stare at us with unwinking, beady eyes. Plump short tailed meadowlarks swooped from rosebush to rosebush trilling their farewell autumn song.

Our wide, shallow valley at that time was

mostly open range, covered with short wiry grass and buckbrush, with a few scrubby poplars and willows huddled in the coulees along the creek banks. Far to the west the blue Rockies made a jagged edge above the shimmering horizon. Here and there were shallow sloughs, now half empty, and ducks, mallards, teal, and pintails, sailed placidly among the reeds that fringed the shores. Red winged blackbirds, gathering for their fall migration whirled excitedly about us, and set up an indignant chirring as we passed. The trail which wandered up and down the rolling slopes was nothing more than two ruts, made by the wheels of wagons and democrats, and the hooves of the teams that pulled them. The shallower rut in the middle was made by the single horses that pulled the lighter buggies.

The sun was growing hot as we topped the ridge on the south side of the valley, and the horses showed sweat patches on their necks and flanks. The hot, still air was tangy with the scent of dry grass and prairie lavender. The gaudy gaillardias, mauve Michaelmas daisies, and golden rod, made patches of bright embroidery on the grey green homespun of the prairie.

A couple of miles farther and the plateau of the ridge sloped away again. The little town of Strathmore came into view, a cluster of buildings and a row of red grain elevators strung out along the railroad track. Soon we bumped over the track and passed the dingy little station house, drove up the dusty main street, one short block of little stores with flat, false fronts, the weather beaten hotel and post office, to the livery barn. The horses were put up, then there was just time to walk back to the station.

The train from the east had already sent out its warning whistle from a few miles down the track, that whistle that has meant so much to so many lonely souls, the homesick immigrants on the farms, the cowboys on the ranges, and the homesteaders. That banshee wail that blasted through the winter blizzards, the thrilling lilt on a

moonlit summer night, bringing to some, nostalgic
memories, to some the surging hope of release
from exile, and to some a comforting reminder
that there was a thread stretching across the
long miles, a link with another world and, in
many cases, happier days.

The train came panting up to the platform,
its bell ringing furiously, and the station
master appeared, black waistcoat unbuttoned over
his white shirt, black sateen arm protectors, and
green eyeshade, to hand a sheaf of papers to the
blue overalled driver, who leaned out of his cab
to take them. We climbed aboard and found a seat
in the day coach, as milk cans, freight, crates
of poultry, mailbags, and parcels were loaded and
unloaded, and then, with bell ringing and another
long drawn out blast of its whistle, the engine
strained forward with much jolting and squealing,
until the wheels bit into the rails.

"Now we're off!" Father took off his peanut
straw hat, and wiped his forehead. We sat on a
green plush seat and I listened to the clacketty
clack of the rails, hugging my excitement to
myself. Father chatted with a couple in the
opposite seat, and I watched the green gold
prairie slipping quickly past. We stopped at
Cheadle, Langdon, Shepard, little groups of
weathered buildings huddled together, with the
usual red elevator or two along the track. At
each stop was the same flurry of excitement,
shouts and laughter, as baggage of all kinds was
dumped off and taken on, always with the background accompaniment of hissing steam, clanging
bell, and shrilling whistle.

The train was crowded with farmers and
ranchers, with their wives and children, Indians
and their squaws, all going up to Calgary for the
Stampede. Paper parcels of lunch were opened,
sandwiches, large wedges of layer cake, and
bottles of cold tea, and the newsboy did a brisk
trade with oranges, bananas, and chocolate bars.

Soon we were pulling into Calgary station and
then the passengers were crowding out onto the

platform and into the cavernous gloom of the
large waiting room. People were bustling about
and there was a pervading air of excitement and
anticipation. Men in cowboy hats, bright silk
shirts, with handkerchiefs tied about their
necks, farmers in blue or khaki overalls, women
in long cotton dresses, black buttoned boots, and
large straw, flower trimmed hats, and round eyed
children of all ages, streamed out of the cool
dimness of the station into the bright sunshine
of the street.

At that time, around the walls of the Calgary
C.P.R. waiting room, were large flat glass cases
in which were beautiful and imaginative arrangements of dried wheat, barley, oats and flax
spread out on a pale green background. I doubt if
much attention was paid to this fine display on
that exciting day of the Stampede, but the
clever, artistic arrangements were likened to the
village craft of "corn dollies" to be seen in
rural England in days gone by.

Calgary was still a cow town then, still on
the frontier, though the immigrants from the
United States and Britain were flocking in. There
was an abounding feeling of newness and excitement, of adventure and enterprise. Businesses
were being opened up daily, and the song of the
saw and the hammer was heard from dawn till dark,
as houses and buildings of all sorts went up
almost overnight.

We hurried along with the crowd towards the
exhibition grounds. Now and then light gusts of
wind funneled down the Bow Valley from the west,
but it was unusually hot and close. Buggies and
wagons, men on horseback, a few cars, and men,
women and children on foot, were all heading in
the same direction.

"They say there is a flying machine!" said
Father excitedly, adjusting his wide brimmed
straw hat at a jaunty angle.

"A flying machine! Does it fly? With people
in it?" I asked incredulously.

"Wait and see." answered Father, with the

stock reply of a grownup who doesn't know the answer.

We visited the exhibition building, where displays of farm implements were set up, and where there was a row of stalls selling various goods. I collected free samples of soap, and biscuits, and other treasures. The stock barns, fragrant with the scent of hay, grain sheaves, and saddlesoap, were full of stamping horses, with manes and tails braided with bright ribbons; fat cattle, sheep, pigs and poultry. Outside the air was now oppressive, and the dust rose in clouds. Men wiped the perspiration off their faces with red spotted bandannas, women fanned themselves with cardboard fans on sticks, and I was glad I had my sunbonnet.

We pushed our way through the throng to the tiered rows of rough plank seats which served as the grandstand, and Father bought tickets. Finding seats was a problem, but we finally struggled over a row of feet and skirts and knees, to a vacant length of plank.

"I beg your pardon, Madam!" Father kept repeating with a courtly wave of his straw hat. "I am so sorry!" as he tramped on patent leather toecaps.

Finally we settled down thankfully on the hard boards. Each row of seats served as a foot rest for the seats behind, so it was impossible to avoid wiping one's dusty boots on the dresses and trousers of those in front of us, and in turn having the boots of those behind wiped on us.

Somewhere below us a band was playing. A little group of people appeared from behind the grandstand and mounted a low platform in front of the stand. Somebody, no doubt His Excellency the Duke of Connaught, made a short speech which was completely inaudible but was cheered vociferously by the crowd.

Now we had time to look about us. There was a corral where the bucking and roping exhibitions would take place, and a race track where the chuckwagon races would be run. Over to the right and beyond the track was a group of tepees and tents, and a little distance from the stand we could see a small roped off enclosure. In the centre of this was a strange looking thing, rather like a double winged kite.

"There it is!" Father exclaimed, pointing at the enclosure. "That's the flying machine."

The flimsy looking contraption was a biplane, the upper and lower wings strung together with criss crossing wires, and the wheels on which it rested were like the wheels of Mother's bicycle which had come out from England with us. In front of the wings was a sort of bucket seat with levers on each side, and as far as I could see there was nothing in front or under the seat. I wondered what it would feel like to soar up into the air with one's feet dangling out over nothing.

I have been unable to find any record of any kind of aircraft being on display at the Calgary Stampede in 1912, and it is possible that this so called flying machine was some sort of replica of the 1912 biplane that was the current "Wonder of the World".

Harry Petter was enormously interested in the specimen on display that day and talked of it often afterwards. Before we came to Canada his twin brothers Ernest and Percy, both inventive engineers of the firm of Petter Engines Limited in Yeovil, were experimenting with flying machines, and later bought a large property outside Yeovil, on which the Westland Aircraft Works was built. During the first world war the firm built many of the famous fighter aircraft, for the Government. One of the first seaplanes ever engaged in naval warfare was designed and built by Westland Works, and this plane was attached to the battleship H.M.S. Lion in the Battle of Jutland on May 31, 1916.

A bareback pony race was being run off. It was a motley lot of Indian ponies that were strung out along the track, buckskins, roans, piebalds, and skewbalds, the bucks riding them

dressed in gaudy shirts, fringed chaps and bright
neckerchiefs. Some wore their long hair tied
back, some wore headbands, and the toes of their
beaded mocccasins were clamped under the horses'
stomachs. There was much shrill yipping and
shouting from the bucks and squaws lining the
fence, and the whites laughed and cheered.

We watched the bucking and roping
contests,but I hated the cruelty of the branding
exhibition, and seeing the terrified calves being
roped, and dragged about the dusty corral by
their necks. I even felt a horrified sort of
satisfaction, when one of the cowboys was bucked
off, kicked by his frantic horse, and had to be
carried off unconscious.

There was still no sign of the flying machine
going up. Men and boys were standing round the
enclosure, and a man in a long white dust coat,
cap and goggles was waving his arms, talking and
obviously answering questions, explaining this
new marvel to them.

"When is it going up?" people were asking
each other.

"Probably too much wind." somebody said.

The wind had risen a little, and now and
then small, teetering whirlwinds of dust drifted
across the racetrack, but the air became more
oppressive as the afternoon wore on. A low
rumbling suddenly made itself heard above the
noise and shouting, and we noticed that great,
purple thunderheads were building up from the
north west. People began to thread their way
along the seats, and down the steps, and then
suddenly the storm was upon us. A fierce gust of
wind raised choking clouds of dust. Paper, hats,
and everything it could pry loose swirled up into
the air. A blinding flash, a deafening crack of
thunder, and then fine white hail slashed down on
our heads. The stands emptied in a few minutes,
as everybody rushed for shelter, and the Indians
disappeared into their tepees. The hail turned to
rain, beating down in great sheets that churned
the dust to mud in minutes, and water was soon

lying ankle deep in puddles all over the grounds.

"The flying machine!" I cried suddenly, as we splashed through the grounds. "It never went up!"

"Too bad." said Father. "I don't suppose it would be safe to fly it unless the air is quite still."

A tall man with a drooping mustache, well stained with tobacco juice, the water dripping off his cowboy hat, was walking beside us.

"Aw! that thing couldn't fly!" He spat a brown stream of tobacco juice into a puddle. "It's wings don't flap." He waved his arms up and down like a bird in flight. "Wouldn't catch me sitting in that little seat and sailing up into the sky!" He grinned and winked at Father as we hurried on.

The rain stopped as suddenly as it had started, and the sun broke through the scattering clouds. It was much cooler and the air, washed clean of dust, was now so fresh and sweet. We walked back to the town and found a small hotel near the station. We went into the dark, fusty foyer and Father showed me where the washroom was. I did the best I could with my damp hair, and washed my face and hands, smoothed my wrinkled dress, and pulled up my black, ribbed cotton stockings. He was waiting for me when I came out, and as we went into the diningroom I sniffed the fragrance of food and realized how hungry I was. I remember that delicious meal to this day, ham and eggs, fried to perfection, toast dripping with butter, dried apple pie and coffee, the standard suppertime fare in all the restaurants, cafes, and hotels of that day, but how good it tasted and smelled.

Suddenly Father pulled out his watch. "We'll have to run for it! Pick up your things while I pay the bill."

I gathered up my collection of samples and souvenirs and my bedraggled sun-bonnet. Father picked up an armful of bags and parcels containing presents for Mother and the girls, and we hurried out of the hotel. As we ran towards the station, two men were coming towards us along the board sidewalk, and one shouted after us as we raced past.

"It's no use running, no train tonight, washout on the line!"

Father hesitated for a moment then ran on. That could have been true, but it might also have been the sort of joke that was pulled on many an unsuspecting newcomer in those days. The Englishman was fair game, and fell foul of many such tricks until he grew wary.

At the station we found a crowd of tired and worried travellers standing about. It was a fact, there had been a washout. The sudden storm had sent a flash flood down a small creek a few miles to the east, and a bridge had been washed out. There would be no train out that night. A crew was already out working on the site, and it was hoped the train would be able to leave in the morning.

Father was fishing some coins out of his trouser pocket and a comical look of consternation spread over his face.

"A fifty cent piece, two dimes, and a nickel! That won't pay for a hotel room, and breakfast!"

I had a vision of our sleeping out on the prairie, one of my ambitions since hearing about a young girl who had lost her way when walking home alone one summer night. She had managed to sleep comfortably, tucked into a handy haystack and was none the worse except for a few mosquito bites. Looking rather worried, Father went up to a stout man in a blue uniform, who turned out to be the conductor on the delayed train, which was standing in the yards outside the station.

"Tell you what," he said kindly, after our predicament had been explained to him. "You come back in an hour. I'll be locking up then. You and the child can slip into the day coach and I'll lock you in. Mind, if you're caught you must say you sneaked in by yourselves. I'd lose my job if I were blamed for letting you in!"

Father thanked him. I didn't mind too much,

it was almost as exciting to sleep locked up in a railway coach as out on the dark prairie. We wandered about the streets for a while and then returned to the station, which was now almost deserted. It was growing dark and a little chilly as we walked through the empty waiting room, and out into the yards. A dark form beckoned us towards the back of the train and in another minute we were stumbling into the dark, musty interior of the coach. We could just make out the outlines of the empty seats against the dim, grey squares of the little windows.

"You'll have to manage without any light, but it won't be quite dark for a little. You can use the washroom but you mustn't open the windows. I'll be back about seven in the morning and I'll let you out to get some breakfast. If the bridge is repaired the train will pull out at eight."

He left us and we heard the door clang shut. We watched his railwayman's coal oil lantern bob away towards the station building.

"Locked up for the night!" chuckled Father "I wonder what your Mother will say to that when we tell her tomorrow?"

It was hot and stuffy in the coach, but we made ourselves fairly comfortable on the plush seats. Father had a last cigarette and I watched the tip glowing, fading and glowing again, and smiffed the fragrance of the tobacco as I drifted off to sleep.

I woke conscious of being most uncomfortable. It was quite dark and I struggled up still half asleep. I couldn't breathe! There was a horrible smell, and my eyes began to sting, suddenly I was wide awake, the coach seemed to be full of smoke! Father was sleeping peacefully on one seat, with his feet on the opposite seat, and I could just make him out in the gleam of light coming from a lantern hanging somewhere outside. The smoke seemed to be pouring up in a thick column from the seat beside him. I grabbed his arm and shook him as hard as I could.

"Daddy! Daddy! You're all on fire!"

He leaped to his feet and we could see a
glowing, smouldering hole in the seat, and a
surprising amount of smoke pouring up to the
ceiling. He started trying to beat it out, then
ran to the washroom and came back with a tin cup
of water. It was soon out, and the damage was
small, considering the amount of smoke that
filled the coach. Father managed to pry a couple
of windows open an inch or two and a fresh breath
of air wafted through the coach, which made
breathing easier, and I could now see his white
face in the faint light. We didn't sleep much for
the rest of that night, and as I sat curled up
beside Father I could feel him trembling
slightly.

We watched as the dark turned to grey and the
dawn gradually lightened in the east. The smoke
had almost cleared away, and Father remembering
the conductor's warning, carefully shut the
windows. We examined the damage to the seat and
as the hole made by Father's smouldering cigarette was only one of many tears and holes in the
stained and worn plush seat cover, our situation
didn't seem as serious as it had in the dark of
the night.

It was broad daylight when the stout conductor, true to his promise, unlocked the door,
and let us out into the fresh morning air. If he
noticed any smell of smoke he said nothing. We
found a little cafe near the station, and
Father's seventy five cents bought us a satis-
fying breakfast of porridge, eggs, toast and
coffee.

We were home at last, late the following day.
Mother had not been worried, as the young man who
was working for us at that time had ridden to
town the evening before, and heard about the
washed out bridge. In any case, Father's comings
and goings were so often uncertain and unpre-
dictable, that she probably would not have been
too concerned.

I was too enthralled with my own story of our
adventures, as I boasted and bragged to my

sisters of all we had seen and done, to notice
how Mother reacted, when she heard that we had
been locked up for the night. I had been warned
not to mention the near disaster we had in the
railway coach, and I doubt if anybody ever heard
of that one event of our trip to the first
Calgary Stampede.

Father and Joan, ready for an adventure

Calgary General Hospital

It was Saturday morning and I was feeling very peculiar. I had set out to walk the two miles to the Worthington's farm, to pick up our mail, which they had promised to bring out from Strathmore the day before. We had an agreement with them by which a member of each family would collect the other's mail when in town, and each family had a spare key to the other's mail box. At that time, there was no town or rural delivery and the settlers had to fetch their mail from the town post offices. The Strathmore post office served a large area and one end of the sunny little room was lined with the metal mailboxes from floor to ceiling.

My tenth birthday was a couple of weeks away, when on this cold November morning I started out, well bundled up in coat, wool toque, scarf, overshoes and mitts. Somehow I couldn't make my legs walk in a straight line, and my head ached. I reached the barbed wire fence along the road allowance opposite our gate, and as I bent over to crawl under the wire, a sudden sharp pain stabbed through my stomach. I grabbed the fence post and slowly sat down on the frozen ground. The pain eased after a minute or two, and I looked up at our tall red painted house standing on its little hill some hundred yards away. It was doing strange things, it seemed to slowly sway from side to side, and the roof bulged in and out.

Across the road in our pasture, horses stamped and pawed the hard frozen ground as they nibbled at the frosty grass, and I could hear the pigs in their sty rooting and grunting. The winter sun was low in the south, the pale sky cloudless but hazy. I sat for a minute or two. As the dull throb in my stomach eased, I pulled myself up and started slowly back towards the house, not quite sure what was happening to me. But I realized that I couldn't walk those miles to the neighbour's farm.

"The child is poorly." Mother said as she felt my forehead. "Take her upstairs, Dorothy, and put her in the fluffy bed."(Dorothy Evans, daughter of a newly arrived English settler, was at that time Mother's helper, and when she had any spare time, our governess.)

As children we were never fussed over, mere colds, upset stomachs, bumps and bruises were ignored, and we survived them with the least possible commotion, and few complaints. In an alcove in our parents' bedroom was a large cot with high iron railings, and in this was a feather mattress, so thick and plump with feathers, that one sank deeply into it. This was used for any child who was ill enough to need special attention, and to be allowed to sleep in it, was worth almost any inconvenient illness.

During that night I was alternately blazing hot, or freezing cold, and strange dreams raced through my head. Now and then Mother's face floated over me in the darkness. The next day somebody fetched Dr. Girvin from Strathmore, and he diagnosed inflammation of the bowel, as appendicitis was called in those days. Sometime in the early years of this century, King Edward VII had his appendix removed by a team of famous Harley Street surgeons, and from that time on inflammation of the bowel was given the more dignified name of appendicitis.

The doctor decreed that I must be taken immediately to Calgary, as an operation would have to be performed within hours, if my life were to be saved. I don't remember much about the trip into town, but I was laid on the bottom of a sleigh and covered with rugs. There was little snow to cushion the holes and ruts, and every jolt of the runners echoed in my insides. Mother and Father were with me, and we caught the afternoon train for Calgary. There were no berths on the train, but a kindly guard found an extra seat which was laid across a two seat compartment, and I was laid on it. The train was crowded, and nearby somebody was peeling an orange. The strong pungent smell seemed to clear my head a little.

Somebody must have notified the Hospital that a patient was on the way, as two men with a stretcher were waiting on the platform, when the train pulled into Calgary station. I was carried shoulder high through the crowded waiting room as the men kept shouting "Way for the ambulance!" "Way for the ambulance!" I felt very important as interested faces drifted past the stretcher.

I was operated on as soon as possible. The appendix had burst, and peritonitis had developed which complicated things. To make a complete nuisance of myself to the doctors, nurses and the entire hospital management, four days after the operation I developed scarlet fever. Nobody expected me to survive, but I was a very stubborn type. There was an isolation hospital in Calgary at that time, and I would have been sent there, if it weren't for the critical condition of peritonitis, and the festoons of tubes that seemed to reach in all directions from my tummy.

I was isolated together with a pretty, curly haired young nurse, in one large ward, and we were shut in there together for six weeks. The doctors, shrouded in floor length white gowns, caps and gloves, visited me frequently, and I felt that I was considered a special sort of patient. In fact, I was enormously spoiled and petted. However, I was a bit abashed one day when I was on the way to recovery, when one of the doctors sat on the side of my bed and wagged a finger at me.

"Joan, do you like raisins?" I nodded. "Do you eat a lot of them?" I lay still for a moment, suddenly recollecting the handsful I had sneaked into my mouth when I was supposed to be stoning them for Mother's baking. The doctor frowned at me, pulling his bushy eyebrows down over his twinkling blue eyes.

"Well, Joan, be sure and see that they are all stoned before you eat them after this. Your appendix was stuffed full of raisin stones, and that is what brought on your appendicitis! I am afraid you must have been sneaking them out of your Mother's store cupboard."

Christmas came and the staff sent in a stocking stuffed with all kinds of toys and books, and as by that time, I was allowed some solid food again, there was roast turkey and trimmings on my tray, but no plum pudding. Somebody put a little Father Christmas in one corner of the tray, with a sprig of holly.

Eventually, the peeling process due to the scarlet fever cleared up, and it was considered safe to move me out of the ward, so that it could be disinfected. I was still pretty weak, and the first time I was allowed to stand up, my legs gave way, and I collapsed into a heap on the floor, to my consternation and annoyance.

At last Father came up to Calgary to take me home, and we took the train down to Ardenode where Roy, our farm help at that time, was to meet us. It was very cold, and the snow was in deep drifts. I had been warmly dressed with extra clothes which Mother had sent up with Father, and a pair of thick, grey, fleeced pants, knickers we called them, were pulled well up under my dress. These were fastened at the waist with buttons, and the baggy legs were long, and buttoned below my knees.

When the train pulled into the station, Father lifted me down the steps, and Roy took one arm and Father the other, to help me along the platform, to where the team and wagon box on runners were waiting. Unfortunately, the button holding up the knickers came undone, and suddenly they flopped down around my feet. Due to the bands buttoned tightly around my knees, I couldn't step out of them, and I was well and truly hobbled. Ranchers, cowboys and farmhands, with wide grins on their faces stood along the platform, and laughing faces peered out of the train windows, as I scuffled, and Father and Roy tried to unravel me. Then Roy lifted me by one elbow, and Father the other, and they carried me the rest of the way, with the disgusting knickers dragging behind me over the snow. I was abysmally mortified, and when they lifted me up and dropped me over the side of the wagon box, in which we were to make the long drive to Radfords, I dived down under the rugs and managed to pull the bulky pants up under my dress to my waist, and got the button into the button hole once more.

It was wonderful to be home again. As we entered the warm kitchen, the twins, then about four and a half, were standing just inside the door, and they stared solemnly at me. Betty and Barbara helped me off with my outdoor clothes, curious to see what I looked like, after all those weeks in the hospital. Mother hugged me, and rubbed my cold hands.

Father had made a little white painted wooden dressing table and stool, to stand beside my bed, and Mother had sewn a dainty flounce to go round the table. It was a very happy homecoming.

Betty and Joan.

Trip to Horseshoe Canyon

On his trips to Carbon and Drumheller for supplies of coal, Father had become intrigued with the fascinating and weird formations of the Badlands of Red Deer River Valley, and especially with the stories of exploration teams of archaeologists having recently discovered dinosaur fossils, and prehistoric artifacts, in the cutbanks of the Red Deer river

A few miles west of Drumheller is the Horseshoe Canyon, a wide, semi-circular sweep of valley, its steep banks deeply eroded, curving south from the Red Deer river like an enormous horseshoe. Within this canyon, are several sections of good farmland, on a level with the flat surrounding prairie. Father heard that a half section of unbroken land, within the southern curve of the canyon, was for sale, and he decided that he should drive up and have a look at it.

At this time Father had a middle aged Swede working for him. John Johnson, he pronounced it "Yon Yohnson", was a tall, fair haired, middle aged man, quiet and gentle, kind to both animals and humans. Mother liked and trusted him, and he was so reliable and competent, that Father had no qualms about leaving him in charge of the family and Radfords for a few days.

And so, some time in the late fall, when the crops were in and the threshing finished, Father and I started out one grey, chilly day, with a wagon and team of work horses for the forty mile drive across the prairie. We had with us a supply of food, and plenty of warm bedding, as Father planned that we would camp one night on the way, sleeping in the wagon, and would probably be able to find some sort of accommodation at one of the farms in the area when we arrived.

This was just the sort of adventure that Father loved, a grand sort of escapade, with never a doubt that anything might go wrong.

I was about eleven at the time, and just as excited and confident as he was. My schooling at this time did not interfere with the expedition, as Betty, Barbara and I, were enjoying a holiday interlude between governesses and St. Hilda's College in Calgary, where we were to be enrolled as boarders the following spring.

The days were growing short, and as we drove along, the unbroken grey sky seemed to close down upon us. It was still, but not very cold, and the horses plodded along the rutted trail, as it wound up and down over the undulating country. In the early afternoon, when we were several miles on the way, we noticed a few flakes of snow drifting quietly down, and settling gently on the short dry grass. They fell faster and faster, and before long the ground whitened, and the shallow ruts of the trail grew faint, as the snow filled them in.

There were few farmsteads in that area at that time, and we could see no sign of life anywhere in the failing light. The unbroken prairie all about us was completely deserted, and we were very much alone. Father pulled the team to a stop, and we looked around at the quiet, shrouded landscape. After a minute he started considering the situation out loud - "Perhaps we should turn back - but we are well on our way - in any case we won't be able to get back to Radfords tonight - possibly the storm will blow over shortly?" Eventually he decided we should go on. He slapped the reins on the horses' rumps and they again leaned into their collars, the wagon creaked, and the wheels scrunched into the new snow which was freezing hard as it fell.

By the time we reached the cutbanks of the Rosebud Creek it was almost dusk, and the snow was still falling softly. With a bit of a shock we realized that somehow we had missed the trail, the creek cutbanks fell sharply away from the level prairie ahead of us, and there was no sign of the track that should have led us down to where we could ford the creek.

The snow was now three or four inches deep, and Father decided that the only thing for us to do, was to stay where we were for the night. When daylight came, we would hopefully be able to find our way down to the flats. He unhitched the horses, and tied them to the wagon wheels, put horseblankets on them, and gave each an oatsheaf. He spread a large tarpaulin over top of the wagon, and pulled it out and down to the ground along one side. Then he hammered in a couple of short stakes, and tied the corners of the tarpaulin tightly to them. We brushed the snow off the ground, and under this shelter we sat on a blanket, and ate a cold supper of bread and butter and meat, and drank milk out of a cream can. We joked and laughed like a couple of runaway school children, and I cannot remember that I had the slightest qualm that we were in any kind of predicament.

The snow had stopped but it was growing colder, and the snow was now frozen hard. We were dressed warmly with thick Mackinaw coats, and I had a heavy knitted wool toque shaped like a cone with a large tassel on the peak which hung down my back. These toques were worn by women and children at that time, and we nicknamed them "jellybags" after the bags used to strain fruit juices. Father wore his muskrat fur cap with the earflaps down, and we both had the large fleece lined black overshoes with metal clasps up the front, that everbody wore in wintertime in those days.

We were to sleep in the wagon, fully dressed and rolled up in blankets, and with the tarpaulin stretched over the top of the wagon box we would be well protected. Father lit a coal oil stable lantern, and hung it at one end of the wagon box under the tarpaulin, and the heat from this would give a little warmth to our makeshift shelter.

Then he said he would walk along the top of the cutbank for a little way, and see if he could locate the trail, and that I could curl up in the wagon until he got back. With the horses to keep me company I wasn't the least bit nervous, and after watching Father walk slowly away into the night I tucked myself up comfortably, and was soon feeling drowsy.

Night had now fallen, but it wasn't really dark. The fresh white snow gleamed coldly under the ink black sky. The patient horses had finished their oatsheaves, and stood quietly, occasionally shifting from one foot to the other. I was glad of their peaceful presence. I think I slept for a while, then woke suddenly, and realized that Father had not returned. I pulled one end of the tarpaulin back, and stood up with a sudden feeling of alarm, wondering if something could have happened to him. I stared out along the line of the winding cutbank in the direction he had gone, but could see nothing. I began to wonder if I should try to go and find him if he didn't return. Was he wandering about, lost, could he have fallen and hurt himself? But just then with a great throb of relief, I saw his dark form clambering over the edge of the bank, and in another minute he was shaking the snow off his overshoes and climbing into the wagon. He told me that he had found his way down one of the scrubby coulees onto the flats, but had not been able to see any sign of the trail or the ford. However, he had seen, far along the valley, a faint gleam of lamplight, so we would probably be able to get help in finding our direction in the morning. Then we pulled the tarpaulin back over the top of the wagon, and rolled up in our blankets, slept peacefully until morning.

When daylight came, we found it had turned a little milder, and the snow showed signs of softening. We drove on along the cutbank, and soon found a track leading us down to the ford. We must have surprised the rancher and his wife when we drove up to their door a little later, as it was still very early, but they took us in and gave us a wonderful breakfast. I can still remember the rich smell of the home cured bacon, the slabs of homemade bread toasting on the top of the range, and the coffee. Afterwards the rancher and Father rolled themselves cigarettes from little drawstring bags of ZigZag tobacco, and sat talking beside the heater for some time. Soon, we were on our way again, but we had lost so much time that by late afternoon we were still a long way from the Horseshoe Canyon. Here the smooth grassland prairie curved up and down, into low mounded hills and ridges, and the trail wound about and over them.

The sky was still overcast and there was no wind, but the air was chilly, and traces of snow lay here and there in the hollows. The light was fading once again, and the horses were showing signs of fatigue, when we saw a low, rather ramshackle building on the side of a little hill, with a wisp of smoke curling up from the black stovepipe sticking through the roof. Father drew up, handed me the reins, climbed down and knocked on the door. It opened immediately, and a tall middle aged man stood in the doorway. Behind him was a little stout woman, and looking out between the man's legs and round the woman's skirts, were four round faced children. Father explained our predicament and asked if they could put us up for the night. We were immediately invited in, and made welcome, but it must have been a problem to find room for two extra in that one room shack.

As we found out later, this American family had driven up from one of the central States earlier that year and taken up their homestead. The man built the little home, and the small stable for their few animals single handed. The house consisted of one long room, and at each end, from wall to wall, was a boarded enclosure about three feet high, and some six feet wide. These, filled with straw, packed down hard, and covered with grey blankets, served the family for beds, the man and his wife sleeping in one, and the four children in the other. They had very little furniture, most of it made by the home-steader out of rough lumber and wooden crates. It was arranged that the two men would sleep in the stable, and that I should sleep in the straw bed with the wife, and this seemed quite satisfactory to all.

I don't remember what we had for supper, but Father when recounting the story later, said the American had told him, that when they had arrived in Canada they had had no money, but that he had found enough work in Drumheller to buy lumber for the house, and a good cookstove, and a few necessities. He also told Father that the only groceries they bought, were flour, and the large wooden buckets of plum and apple jam, that were a stock commodity in any general store in those days. The wife baked the sourdough bread, and they ate it with the jam. Other than that, their food was what he could shoot, prairie chickens, ducks and jackrabbits. If I remember correctly, they had one or two cows, and so probably had a good supply of milk and butter.

The children ranged in age from about four to ten, the oldest a couple of years younger than I. We were tremendously interested in each other. I can remember the four of them standing in a row staring at me with solemn faces and large round eyes, saying not a word. I watched them being tucked into their wood and straw bed, two at the top and two at the bottom, and then I partly undressed and clambered into the bed at the other end of the room, It was surprisingly comfortable, and wrapped in the heavy grey blankets, I was soon drowsy. Father, the man and his wife, sat around the cookstove, talking for a long time, and their voices wove back and forth into my dreams.

I cannot remember the name of this little family, nor anything of what happened to them in later years, but I have never forgotten their kindness and generosity to us on that cold wintry day, despite their meagre circumstances. At that time, of course, on the remote and often isolated homesteads, it was an exciting event when a stranger appeared, and it was unthinkable not to offer hospitality to the passing traveller, no matter how limited one's means were.

The following day we continued on our way and eventually arrived at the Horseshoe Canyon. As we approached, the road wound along the rim of the Canyon, and we gazed down with amazement at the five hundred foot cliffs that dropped down from the level prairie. We were fascinated by the weird formations of this strange wind and water eroded valley, the ridged columns of the hoo-doos rising up here and there from the sandy floor where little grew, but small, twisted, prickly cacti, now dry and brown.

We stayed that night at another farmhouse, this time with an older couple. Father knew this farmer, and it was he who had interested him in the property inside the Canyon. The farm, a short distance south of the canyon, was large, with a comfortable house and large barns and outhouses, everything well arranged and prosperous looking, with many well fed horses and cattle standing around the corrals, and chickens, ducks and geese, clucking and quacking about the farmyard. There was a tall metal windmill whirling merrily away behind the house, keeping the water troughs filled and supplying the house. If I remember correctly the farmer's name was DeWett, and they were probably of Dutch origin. Their house was immaculate, the barns clean and sweet smelling, and the whole homestead bespoke good management and well being.

The next morning Mr. DeWett drove us across to the canyon, and we followed a road that wound down through a shallower part of the valley, and up the opposite bank to the half section that was for sale. He took us to the edge of the canyon, and climbing down a few feet he kicked at the sandy soil, and scraping away a few inches, showed us a deep layer of the soft, black coal that is found in abundance in that area. He also told us that in spring and summer there were many rattle snakes in the sandy banks and coulees, and that rather cooled my enthusiasm for exploring for dinosaur fossils and prehistoric artifacts.

The rest of this adventure is rather vague in my memory, but I remember we took another route on our homeward journey, staying overnight in a little rooming house at Rockyford, and making the trip in two days. All was well when we arrived at Radfords, and no doubt we made the most of our experiences when describing them to all and sundry.

Eventually Father bought this half section, and later on built a bungalow and barns on it. For a couple of years he successfully farmed it and Radfords, with the help of Mr. Johnson and other hired men. By this time he had acquired a second hand Model T Ford, and as some road allowances, and even a few stretches of graded roads had appeared between Strathmore and Drumheller, travelling between farms was a much easier undertaking.

Surrey With the Fringe on Top

After the great influx of colonists during the early years of this century, and before the outbreak of the First World War, some of the settlers, and especially the older ones, were finding that their dream of the wonderful new life in the Land of Promise had become something of a nightmare. Their animals died from lack of proper care, the farm implements on which they had spent so much of their capital broke down, and they were unable to cope with the dawn to dark heavy work during the busy seasons. Many sadly had to give up, and move into the towns to find work, or go back to Britain or the States. So there were often auction sales on these farms.

Father sometimes drove out to these sales and would come home with a variety of bargains, a couple of piglets, a piece of neglected farm machinery, a chair, or perhaps some family heirloom, that had had to be discarded. On one occasion he bought an ancient copper warming pan with a long carved handle for which he had paid fifty cents.

One day he arrived home from a sale with a four wheel vehicle hitched to the back of his buggy. It was old and fragile, but beautifully made, the spokes of the large wheels spindly but strong. There were two comfortable double seats, leather covered and well padded, with high backs and arm rests. Perched high on the body and over all was a canopy from which hung a lacy fringe. All the original paint or varnish had weathered away, but Father scraped and sanded it and then lovingly refinished it.

On a fine hot summer's day Betty and I were off to Strathmore, with a long list of groceries to be picked up at the General Store.(It was probably during the summer of 1914, when Betty was ten and I twelve). During the school holidays, we took on many such tasks to help out during the busy season. We were wearing our going-to-town clothes, cotton dresses, long

black ribbed stockings, black laced leather boots
and floppy straw hats. We had Kitty and Maud
hitched to the new buggy, and it was very pleasant
to sit in the shade of the fringed top, as the
horses trotted sedately along the road which
skirted the construction line. Ahead of us the
prairie rose gradually towards the south, and
beyond this rise, and still out of sight, was the
little town of Strathmore, with its string of red
elevators along the railway line.

The air was very still and along the distant
horizon to the west the heat waves shimmered,
melding land and sky in a misty haze. The sky was
a pale soft blue.

The large wheels spun merrily along. Betty,
sitting on my right, was driving, and her thick
corkscrew curls bobbed up and down as the surrey
bounced on the rough road. Patches of large red,
brown and yellow gaillardias, showed here and
there against the sage brown grass. Bushy clumps
of goldenrod, already breaking out their feathery
yellow blossoms, stood against the barbed wire
fence. A few cows stood knee deep in a slough,
chewing their cud and swishing their tails across
their backs to ward off the flies and mosquitoes.
White and grey sandpipers, tails up-tilted,
darted about in the shallow edges of the pond.

The horses slowed to a walk, their shoulders
showing dark patches of sweat, and Betty pulled
them to a halt to allow them to rest. She pointed
her whip towards the west.

"Look! There's something funny going on over
there. I've been watching it - something moving
in the sky!" I followed the direction of her whip
and could see the filmy heat waves which seemed
to undulate slowly. Betty was right, dark shapes
were forming in the haze, in a line a little
distance above the horizon. As we watched, they
seemed to solidify into squares and oblongs -
buildings? Then a little further to the right, we
could see two or three reddish box like shapes
that seemed to stand on wavery V-shaped bases.
There was something familiar about the strange

panorama that now spread mistily above the horizon.

"It looks like Strathmore, Betty! But why is it over there? And up in the sky?" I looked around at her. She was staring at the shimmery vision.

"It's upside down!" She exclaimed, and then jumped with excitement. "It's a magic lantern! That's what it is!" We had been taken to a magic lantern show at Nightingale School the winter before as a Christmas treat,when shadowy pictures of villages and towns had been shown on a screen. I looked around us and over my shoulder. Nothing there.

"But there's no lantern, Betty!" Undeflated, Betty turned to me and said firmly,

"Then it's magic!" Betty always had the last word.

The upside down vision did not last long. The buildings seemed to tremble, then slide sideways, and grow faint. In a few minutes all that was left was a darkish line in the hazy distance. I thought of the wide grin of the disappearing Cheshire cat in Lewis Carrol's Alice in Wonderland, when as it faded, only the grin was left in the tree.

The horses were becoming restless, as the mosquitoes swarmed around us, and they were settling on us, too. Betty slapped the reins on the horses' rumps, and we started on up the long slope towards the town. When we topped the rise, we were relieved to see Strathmore, still some three miles ahead of us, safely anchored to the ground, right side up, and in the right place, the red elevators and the long, low station buildings in the foreground. Everything looked normal.

We reached town, crossed the railway track, turned right, and drove into the dusty main street. The hitching post in front of the General Store had a heavy metal ring on it. We tied the horses' halters to this, went into the store and handed over our grocery list to be made up, and packed into wooden crates. Then we crossed the street to the Chinese Cafe, for our usual treat of fried egg sandwiches, well laced with HP sauce, and large cups of pale Chinese tea.

We knew the Chinese proprietor well, and decided to tell him about our experience. He was a small man with black hair smoothed back from his round pale face. He ran his cafe single handedly, did all the cooking, serving, washing up, worked long hours seven days a week, was always cheerful, and had a broad smile for everybody. There were four little tables, and one oblong one down the middle, in the small room, and the tiny kitchen was off to the right behind a large serving hatch.

The Chinaman came over to out table and ceremoniously placed the plates of fragrant fried egg sandwiches and hashed brown potatoes in front of us. His stiffly starched apron covered him from his chin to his feet, he smiled down at us.

"We saw something very funny when we were coming into town," I began.

"It was like a picture in the sky," continued Betty. "It was like Strathmore, away over there." She pointed with her arm towards the west. "And it was upside down!"

"Ah, yes." Mr. Chow nodded his head solemnly. "MI-aaage, that light picture. We see it in China too. You ask your Fa-aader - he tell you how it happen."

We often saw hazy distortions on the horizons in those days, when the air was unpolluted and clear. Sometimes, what looked like glassy pools of water, would appear on the dry prairie, and then slowly disappear as one approached. As far as I remember we never again saw a mirage, as clear as that of the upside down Strathmore in the western sky.

J.Ke

St. Hilda's College

School days - school days
Dear old Golden Rule days
Reading and writing and 'rithmetic
Taught to the tune of a hickory stick.

G. Edwards 1907

About 1914 Betty, Tommy and I were enrolled
at St. Hilda's College in Calgary as boarders. In
spite of the difficult times, Mother and Father
decided it was time for us to go to the College.
If I remember correctly, the fee was $50.00 a
term, which covered all schooling, plus music,
sports, etc., and board and lodging.
St. Hilda's was a Church of England school.
At that time there were three private schools in
Calgary, St. Hilda's for girls, Western Canada
College for boys, and Mount Royal School which
was co-educational. All three schools took
boarders. There were about twenty boarders at St,
Hilda's that year, aged six to eighteen. We slept
in two large dormitories, the seniors in one, and
the younger girls in the other.
The first evening we were sitting round the
large table in the school diningroom, having
supper with the other girls, and Tommy was
sitting opposite me. I looked across at her, and
she was stolidly eating her meal, staring down at
her plate, while great tears slowly ran down her
cheeks.We were all homesick of course,but I doubt
if Betty and I, so close to each other,felt the
cruel desolation as keenly as she did.
Miss Shibley, the head mistress, was a tall,
slight woman, rather tense and distant to the
pupils and staff. She had beautiful white hair,
swept up from her forehead in a large roll. She
always wore her long black gown when taking
classes, and she would sweep impressively into
the school room, with it floating out behind her.
She was a fine teacher and lecturer, and took

complete control of her class, as soon as she entered the room. There was never an untoward sound from us and we paid strict attention to her.

The pupils at St. Hilda's took their studies seriously. The mistresses were excellent teachers, and instilled into us the love of learning, making us aware of the importance and need for knowledge. History and literature in particular, were stressed, and the small library was well stocked with books.

The senior girls were often taken to operas, concerts, and plays, as before the days of cinema and television, many fine groups of stage actors and musicians regularly toured Canada and the United States. I remember one particularly exciting evening, when we were taken to see the D'Oyly Carte Company in, "The Mikado", and another when the players from Stratford-on-Avon put on, "As You Like It".

A serious young curate gave us weekly scripture lessons. He was rosy and rotund and his short, fat legs were tight in his trousers. He was painfully self-conscious and we made the sessions difficult for him by asking deliberately stupid, irreverent questions, and he would blush furiously, and and stammer.

Every Sunday the senior girls went to the early Communion service at the Pro Cathedral, and the whole school attended the regular morning service at eleven o'clock. We always walked the half mile there and back, in a crocodile, two and two, the younger girls in front and the older ones behind, with one or two mistresses bringing up the rear. We were ceremoniously paraded up to the pews reserved for us, near the front of the nave. The mistresses sat in the aisle seats, keeping a close watch on our behaviour.

On Saturday afternoons, the older girls were allowed to walk downtown to the shops, and this was the great event of the week. We walked down in a group, in the charge of a mistress. Then we were given permission to split up, and were allowed an hour or so, to do whatever we liked, with the strict admonition, that we were to meet again at a certain time, at a certain place, usually the "rendezvous" on the mezzanine floor of the Hudson's Bay Company Store. We always included a visit to a Greek restaurant on First Street West, for icecream. Our usual choice was banana splits, three large dollops of icecream, one bright pink, one white and one chocolate, arranged on sliced bananas which were laid lengthwise on large, oval glass dishes. This confection was topped with piles of whipped cream, and strawberry jam was poured over the top of that.

We were secretly experimenting with "make-up", and would go into the Five and Ten to examine the boxes of white facepowder, black eyebrow pencils, and scarlet lipstick. We took home free samples, and spent hilarious hours, making each other up, stark white faces, heavy black eyebrows, and scarlet lips, which of course was all washed off, before we dared appear downstairs. Except in theatricals, no "lady" wore makeup in those days.

The gym. classes were very popular. There was a fine large gymnasium with all kinds of sports equipment, and the mistress was a large, jolly, athletic type who dressed in a voluminous pair of dark bloomers, and a middy blouse. She gave us dancing lessons, as well as the usual exercises, and taught us to waltz, foxtrot, and to do the popular Sir Roger de Coverley. Once a year, a group of the older boys from Western Canada College, was invited to a dance at St. Hilda's, and this was of course, an especially exciting occasion. The senior girls of the school, and an equal number of boys, were introduced to each other, and paired off. We were well chaperoned by our mistreses, and one or two masters from the boy's College. Our music teacher played the piano.

In one of my senior years we had a delicious scandal. One of the boarders, a pretty, vivacious, and very popular girl,was caught having an affair with one of the boys. She was found one evening after dark, when she should have been in a classroom doing her homework, on her hands and knees, fishing a note out of the hedge that bordered the front garden of the school. We never heard what was in the note, but it was from one of the Western Canada boys. Our classmate was taken to Miss Shibley's study. It must have been a serious indiscretion, because she was expelled. We missed her, and there were endless rumours about her and her boyfriend, as we speculated and discussed the affair, until the end of that term.

One year in the late spring, we were studying hard for the final exams. I was not feeling very well,my head ached, and I had a sore throat. I went to the matron, she took my temperature, and put me to bed. The next day spots and some blisters appeared, and it was decided I had chickenpox.

There was a crisis meeting of the staff - the final exams for the year were about to start. If the Health Inspector was notified, would he close the school? What about the day scholars? Should all the parents be notified? Would half the pupils come down with the disease? It was a disaster for St. Hilda's, and I was the cause of it! Of course I knew nothing of that, at the time. I was taken up to a large bare room, on the third storey which was used as an infirmary, and put to bed. No doctor came to see me. The matron, who was inclinded to be a bit irritated with ailing students,looked after me. She tied a cloth over her mouth and nose, and always smelled strongly of iodoform.After the first two or three days I was feeling better,though the large spots covered me from head to foot. I was allowed to get up and dress, my school books were brought in to me, and I did some studying, but I was left very much to myself. My meals were carried up on a tray and left on the mat outside the door. A washstand and basin stood in a corner of the room, as there was no bathroom or running water on the third floor of the school. A jug of warm water and a slop pail, were put outside the door every morning. For two weeks I saw nobody but the matron, and spent the days and nights alone. It was a bit boring, but I had plenty of good books to read, and I also had my water-colour paintbox and brushes.

The dormitory was under the roof and a deep, dormer window looked out over the front garden. The white plastered wall arched over the inside of the dormer, and I had an inspiration. I would cheer the place up by painting a border around this archway. I stood on a chair, and painted an entwined arangement of pink and red rosebuds, and curling green leaves around the arch, and the water-coloured paint stood out well on the white plaster. I was cheerfully occupied for hours, and very proud of my work. I forget the reaction when the room was eventually opened again, but the decoration was still there when I finally left St. Hilda's a couple of years later.

Every morning, my breakfast included a large plate of thick porridge, cold and solidified by the time it arrived. I couldn't bring myself to eat it. A small window looked out across a pathway at the side of the school, onto the back garden of a neighbouring house. In it was a large netted chicken run, standing against the high wooden fence that separated the garden from the schoolyard, and a dozen or so large white hens lived in this pen. I would stand on a chair, open the little window, and lob spoonsful of the porridge out over the fence into the run, and the hens would pounce on it. After a couple of mornings of this routine, as soon as I pushed the window open, they fluttered into a little covey aginst the netting, and clucked happily up at me.

Eventually I was released. The spots had almost disappeared. The rest of the class had written their exams, and I was allowed to write mine in Miss Shibley's study. Strangely enough, no other cases of chickenpox had developed, and the school curriculum had continued with no further disruption. I had missed the Speech Day, and closing exercises, and most of the boarders had already left. Whether anybody other than the school staff, the matron and myself knew about my chickenpox I never knew, but of course my parents had been notified, as I found out later when I arrived home for summer holidays.

1917 was my final year at St. Hilda's. To my delight, but some inward consternation, I was given the honour of delivering the Valedictory at the closing exercises. I had done rather well in my final exams, especially in English, and was rather pleased with myself, but I must admit that the war years had diminished the enrollment at the College, so that there were fewer students to compete for the honour. Many of the clergy from the Cathedral, their wives, and parents of the students would be present. It was an impressive, and traditional occasion. Miss Shibley called me into her study, and explained what should be said in a valedictory, told me to write a draft and take it to her, and then I must memorize it.

Miss Shibley then told me, that Mother had written to her to say that she was not well, and that she and Father would not be able to come up for the Speech Day and closing ceremonies. She had sent some money, and asked Miss Shibley to arrange to have somebody take me down to the shops, and buy me a dress for this special occasion.

The following Saturday afternoon the matron and I walked down to the ladies' wear shops on Eighth Avenue. After I had tried on several outfits, she chose a severe navy blue dress, with a plain white collar. I had visualized something quite different - gauzy, frilly, pale pink or blue - a party dress! I was terribly disappointed and downcast. I tried it on later when I was alone in the dormitory, and hated myself in it. My excitement and happy anticipation had vanished. I packed it up again in its many folds of tissue paper, and put it in a drawer, having shown it to nobody.

The following Saturday when the senior class went downtown on the usual shopping expedition, I rolled it up tightly in its wrapping, and tucked it under my arm. Nobody noticed it, and later I managed to slip away to the shop where it had been bought, and found the saleswoman who had sold it to us. I explained that it wouldn't do, and would she please exchange it for something more suitable? She looked a bit suspicious, but I must have been very determined and sure of myself, and she finally gave in. I chose a light blue, flowery voile patterned with pink and mauve, and with a full, billowy skirt. I had to fork out a few more dollars from my pocket money, but it was worth it. My next worry was keeping it out of sight of the matron, until I appeared on the dais. However, my concern was unnecessary, as to my great relief, for some reason she was not in the hall for the great occasion, and I don't remember seeing her again.

Adventure in the Rosebud Valley

In the summer of 1914 Father bought a young Clydesdale stallion from a rancher who lived in the Bow Valley near Shepard, a few miles east of Calgary. Sonsie was a pure-bred, a beautiful pale gold with well feathered fetlocks, a large white star on his broad forehead, and so handsome we all loved him dearly. He had a gentle disposition and always pranced a little when being led or driven.

Mr. Bannister had come out from England about the turn of the century, and now was a prosperous rancher. He, and his wife and family, lived in a comfortable house surrounded with spacious barns and corrals, set on the beautiful grassy flats of the river. Father had had a letter of introduction to him. He helped Father, advising him on stock and implements and befriending us in many ways.

Our mares soon produced some fine foals, and the following year they ran loose with the older horses, on the open range to the south of us. In late summer, one of the men went out to round them up and came back with the older horses, and the bad news that the seven yearlings were not with them.

Father and the farm hands scoured the open prairie for miles around but the seven fillies and geldings had completely vanished. Betty and I, then about ten or twelve years old, and well used to handling horses, rode out one day on Kitty and Maude, heading for the Rosebud Creek area, some six or eight miles to the north east of Radfords.

Over countless years, the creeks and rivers of the foothills and prairies had cut their way from west to east, down from the higher altitudes of the mountains, that are the backbone of the North American Continent. In years of heavy snows and spring floods, the waters over-flow the creek and river beds, eating into the light sandy soil of the prairies, widening and ever widening the shallow valleys. In summertime, as the volume of water lessens, the courses of the shrunken creeks and rivers meander back and forth across the grassy flats between the cut- banks. In southern Alberta, east of the foothills, as the prairie lands flatten, there are no rock formations to contain the waters within cliffs and canyons, and little coulees cut down from the level of the prairie to the creek flats. Scrubby poplars and wolfwillow grow in these coulees, and make good cover for range animals in hot weather, when flies and mosquitoes pester them. There was a chance that our yearlings had broken away from the rest of the horses and were sheltering in the coulees of this little populated area of the Rosebud Creek, and we had hopes we might track them down.

It was hot, the prairie grass was brown and crisp, and grasshoppers, pale green and orange, spurted from the dry grass, crackling their wings as they soared through the hot air. The great dome of the sky, pale as skim milk, was cloudless from horizon to horizon. Gophers popped in and out of their holes, and sat on top of their sandy knolls to watch us go by.

By midday when we reached the Rosebud we were hot, thirsty and hungry. We found a little shade under a poplar, and ate the sandwiches we had brought with us, but we had nothing to drink. The creek bed was almost dry, and we couldn't drink the slimy water. The horses cropped the grass and slupped up the creek water with gusto, making us more thirsty than ever. After a rest we rode on, climbing up the cutbank, so that we could look out over the flat grassy bottom land, through which the creek turned and twisted, hoping that we might spot our horses. Everything was very still, and except for the gophers and grasshoppers, there was no sign of life anywhere, human or animal.

In front of us, the valley took a bend, and we followed a cowpath which cut across a head-land, and there below us, on the far side of the creek bed, we saw a dilapitated log building. It looked deserted, but behind it we saw two saddled horses tied to a post.

"If there's somebody there perhaps they would give us a drink of water." Betty said hopefully. Just then two men emerged from the low doorway. There was something about them that made me a little uneasy.

"Let's go back. I don't like the look of them, Betty - we're a long way from home --"

"Oh, come on! They won't hurt us. Perhaps they've seen the colts. Let's ask them anyway." Kitty and Maud had sighted the two saddle horses behind the shack, and stood with their heads lowered and ears pricked forward. Maud blew gently through her nose and gave a whinny. Obviously they too were curious, and prepared to be friendly, so I gave in reluctantly, and we rode slowly on towards the two figures.

We could see them more clearly now as they leaned against the doorposts, one a little taller than the other, but otherwise very much alike. They seemed old to us, their faces leathery and brown from prairie sun and wind, their shirts, trousers, and wide brimmed hats, all the same sun bleached brown. They continued to stare at us, faces expressionless, and so motionless they might have been carved from the same weathered wood as the old cabin. We forded the creek just below the shack and stopped a little distance from the men, and for a minute nobody said anything. Without any apparent facial effort, a thin stream of tobacco juice squirted from the corner of the mouth of the man nearest to me, and landed squarely on a large stone a couple of yards from him. He slowly raised an arm and wiped his mouth with the back of his hand.

"What you kids doin' out heah?" Betty, always the brave one, spoke up in her clear precise English, her fluting voice confident and assured,

"We're looking for our horses. We've lost seven colts and we wondered if you have seen them?" She smiled sweetly, leaning forward and fluttering her eyelashes appealingly. "We are very thirsty and thought perhaps you would give us a drink of water?" The man who had first spoken swivelled his eyes at me and then back to Betty.

"Where you from, and who's yer Pa? Ain't you a long way from home?"

"Our Father is Mr. James Henry John Bascombe Petter." Betty answered impressively. "And we live at Radfords, which is near Nightingale." There was no answer for a moment, then the man who had not yet spoken took a step forward.

"Gimme that pail, kid, and I'll get yo' a drink. You can get down for a bit, then you better head back home. We ain't seen yo' horses, they ain't anywheres hereabouts." Tied to my saddle ring, I had a five pound lard pail, in which we had carried our sandwiches. I untied it and handed it over. He walked over to a pump and primed it from a bucket standing at one side, then pumped the handle up and down vigorously for some time before the water spouted into the pail. He set it down on the doorstep and went into the dark interior of the cabin and returned a minute later with a bottle of greenish liquid. He poured some of this into the pail, then handed it to Betty. She looked doubtfully into it, then tipped it up and took a sip.

"Oh, that is lovely! Thankyou so much! It's so cold - what did you put into it?" She handed the pail to me and I took a sip. It was ice cold, deliciously sharp and tangy. I gulped greedily, then handed it back to Betty, who drank some more.

"Well, it's lime juice." He held the bottle up and squinted at the label. "Montserrat Lime Juice, bottled in Montserrat. Came all the way from the West Indies, I guess."

The other man was now sitting on the step. Feeling reassured, we had dismounted, and were sitting on the grass. I was now feeling quite friendly towards these kind strangers, who had provided us with such welcome cold drinks. When the last cool drop had trickled down, we climbed back on our horses, and as we gathered up the reins Betty turned to the men.

"We hope you will come and visit us at Radfords some day," she said graciously. The taller man swept off his hat with a flourish and bowed to us.

"Thank you, Ma'am. Maybe we will someday." I had sufficiently recovered from my earlier doubts to say "Yes, please do come, and if you see our colts will you please let us know?"

We said goodbye and started back along the cowpath, the horses heading willingly towards home. The sun was now lowering a little towards the west and a slight breeze had risen which cooled the parched air. As we crested the headland we looked back and saw the men still standing by the doorposts and watching us. We waved and then rode on down the opposite slope towards home.

As we jogged quietly along a cowpath, single file, Betty on Maud in the lead, a sudden thought exploded in my head like a handful of firecrackers - Rustlers! Horse Rustlers! Could those two men be horse thieves, and if so, did they have our yearlings hidden away in some secret place?

Immediately my adventure-story imagination went to work. Yes, of course! That explained the whole queer business. I seethed with excitement. Flooding into my head came stories of adventures in strange lands. I had read my Uncle's Boy's Own Annual stories while staying with Grandmother, stories of brave young boys tracking down ruthless villains, and thwarting brigands and robbers after incredible dangers.

I was soon lost in a world of fantasy. I saw myself creeping through dense jungle as I went, single handed, to rescue our horses and capture the thieves. No that wouldn't do - there wasn't any jungle, the prairie grass was about four inches high and I couldn't stalk brigands through that. Ah! I had it - I would head a posse of red coated Royal Mounted Police. We would surprise

the rustlers just as they were to drive the
horses across the border, capture the thieves and
save our yearlings. Cheers from everybody!

I was jolted back to reality with a bump, as
Kitty stumbled into a gopher hole, and I saw that
Betty, now some distance ahead, had rounded the
corner post of the North Forty, and was heading
down the last half mile of road allowance to
Radfords.

We described our encounter to the family at
suppertime, no doubt making the most of everything. I had not told Betty about my secret
suspicions, and I did not mention them at the
table. I had long since discovered that my
imagination could bring ridicule down upon my
head, and I had learned to hold my tongue on
occasion.

However, later in the evening I found Father
as he was bedding down the horses in the barn.
The evening sun was sending golden beams through
the doorway and dust motes danced in the sweet
hay scented air.

"Daddy, those men, do you know who they could
be?"

"Don't think so, probably horse traders,
plenty of them about. They didn't tell you their
names?"

"No, but they weren't very friendly at first,
I was just a little bit afraid of them." Father
leaned on his fork and looked down at me, his
silvery head haloed against the sunlit western
sky and his blue eyes darkened in the shadow.

"What made you frightened?" he asked.

"I don't know, I felt they didn't like us,
that they didn't like our finding them, I don't
know -" I lowered my voice impressively, "Daddy,
do you think they could be RUSTLERS?"

Father never laughed at my imaginings,
however foolish, and now he stood quietly for a
minute as if he were thinking the possibility
over seriously. Then he said gently,

"Oh, I don't really think so. Rustlers
haven't been reported in this area, and if there

had the police would have sent out warnings, and probaby tracked them down. Too many settlers round here now for rustlers to have much chance." I went to bed that night, reassured, but a little deflated.

Actually during those years there was a good deal of horse and cattle rustling, but mostly along the forty ninth parallel, as American rustlers found it very easy and profitable to slip across the line at night, cut out the best animals from a herd, and drive them back across the border. But there had been few cases of rustling reported in the Strathmore - Nightingale area.

"Truth is stranger than fiction", wrote Lord Byron, in words to that effect, but truth can sometimes be an anticlimax, and that is what happened to my horse rustler theory. How exciting it would have been, if my amazing intuition had brought about the dramatic rescue of our seven horses, and the thrilling capture and conviction of the villainous brigands who had rustled them. I soon found out it was all a dream, the two men were a couple of squatters who had moved into the old cabin.They turned out to be good solid types, brothers whose name I cannot now remember, who were herding a flock of sheep in the Rosebud area. They were away a good deal, shepherding their sheep, and while away always left their cabin open, and stocked with supplies for any travellers who passed by, and needed shelter or food, the traditional frontier hospitality.

Our horses were never found. Actually they may have been rustled, but more likely were unintentionally gathered up during a round-up, by one of the big ranchers, whose large herds of semi-wild horses roamed all over the open range in those days.

The final anticlimax to our Rosebud adventure came a couple of weeks later. We saw two men on horseback riding along the prairie trail to the north of Radfords. They rounded our cornerpost, came down the road allowance and rode up to the house. One of them was leading a small sorrel pony, with a white star on her forehead, and four white fetlocks. Betty and I had seen them as they approached,and recognized them as our "rustlers". They looked just the same, brown and weathered, clothes, boots, faces and hair all the same wind and sun faded colour, as they sat slightly sideways in the heavy, high pummeled stock saddles in the Western Cowboy style.

Father came up and shook hands with them as they dismounted, and they asked if our missing horses had been found. Father shook his head, and explained that they had been missing for some time, and he had little hope they would ever be found. Betty and I were standing there listening, and were already examining the little pony, patting and talking to it, and smoothing its shaggy coat.

The man who held the lead turned to Betty, put the rope into her hand, and said the pony was for us; they had bought it especially for us. I can remember our standing there, staring up at them, quite speechless with delight. Father thanked them but said this was too generous, they must accept some payment. He fished a five dollar bill out of his pocket and handed it to one of the men, who accepted it without comment, and pushed it into his shirt pocket.Betty looked up at him, and asked what the pony's name was. He smiled down at her, looked questioningly at the other man, then said,

"Uh! Oh. I ain't quite sure - lemme see now - Yes! It's Lightning Express. That's it! Lightning Express."

We didn't see it, of course, but I am sure he winked at Father as he spoke.

The little pony was obviously old, and well past her prime, and as we found out would amble patiently along, but didn't like to trot. We loved her dearly, and when she died a couple of years later Father had a deep hole dug, and we held a formal funeral service for her.

Guy Fawkes Day

One November the Worthington family, our nearest neighbours, invited us and others to a skating party and bonfire, on the little lake on their farm, to celebrate Guy Fawkes' Day.

In time Halloween took the place of November fifth as the big fall "fun and high jinks" night, but for the first year or two in Canada, the British colonists remembered Guy Fawkes' Day with the traditional fireworks and bonfires. November Fifth is the anniversary of the infamous attempt in 1605, of a group of conspirators to blow up the Houses of Parliament with gunpowder, and the British have celebrated the foiling of the plot and execution of Guy Fawkes ever since.

Skating on prairie sloughs was usually at its best in late fall after a spell of hard frost, when the sloughs, lakes and creeks were well frozen, and before any heavy snowfall made clearing off the ice difficult. On our neighbour's farm there was a deep little lake which was fed by a spring, and so the water was clean and almost free of the reeds and sludge that filled the shallow sloughs.

On this particular occasion, in early November, conditions were perfect, a few nights of very low temperatures without wind had produced a sheet of fine, smooth ice to a depth of a foot or more. It was planned to build the bonfire in the middle of the little lake. Frozen as hard as it was, and in that cold temperature, it would take a long time for even a fierce fire to melt the ice to any great depth. To make a good base for the fire, the Worthington boys carried buckets of dry soil from a nearby ploughed field, and spread it on the ice in a circle where the bonfire was to be built.

The nearby farmyards were scrounged for every scrap of waste lumber, old wooden crates and boxes, cardboard, anything that would burn. The remains of a deserted log cabin on the banks of the Serviceberry Creek produced some heavy, half rotten logs. During the afternoon the bonfire was carefully built, a fine great pyre, with straw and a few old dry sheaves packed in around the base to make sure the fire got off to a good start.

After an early supper some twenty or thirty people, young and old, from the nearby farms gathered on the lake. The ice was black and gleaming under the starlit sky, and a half moon was riding high. There was no snow, but the ground was sparkling with frost, the grass crisp under our feet.

Father, Betty and I, Roy Frith and Gwen Southwell, had walked over the half mile from Radfords. Mother had stayed home with the younger children, no doubt reluctantly, as she often skated in her younger years.

Roy had recently come out from England to help Father, and to learn prairie farming. He was a tall, good looking man, with bristly fair hair and mustache, and pale blue eyes. Gwen, who had also come out that year, was now our governess, and Mother's right hand assistant. She cheerfully accepted the primitive way of life, made light of the hardships, and brightened the days of all about her. Her thick brown hair was now packed under a large, red wool cap and her brown eyes sparkled with laughter. A romance was blossoming, but nobody suspected it at that time. Roy and Gwen eventually married, and later farmed at Rocky Mountain House.

On this night of the skating party, when everybody had arrived, the fire was lit, and soon the flames were shooting up into the still, frosty air, and the ring of happy, excited faces glowed in the firelight.

Not all had skates, but those without slid and slithered and raced about on the ice, and laughing and shouting, joined hands in a line and pulled each other around in circles. Father and his brothers had learned to skate when they were boys, on the frozen ponds around Yeovil, and now on this prairie lake he was twirling happily around with his hands clasped behind his back, doing figure eights, and I was very proud of him.

I had a pair of skates that had belonged to Mother when she was a girl. A peculiar pair, with large, heavy blades of rusty iron set into wooden platform soles, and with screws protruding upwards through the heels of each, into the heels of my high, laced boots. The skates were then firmly strapped around my ankles and over my insteps. I was very pleased with myself, and although I spent more time sprawled on the ice than actually skating, I had a lot of fun. Betty was managing beautifully on a pair of child's skates with double blades, something similar to roller skates, and on which she was able to navigate much better than I. She was sliding about, bent over double, arms outstretched, with only an occasional fall. Bundled up as we were, in thick coats, wool jerseys, heavy mitts and scarves, we could fall on the ice repeatedly without doing ourselves much harm.

Roy and Gwen were skating together, hand in hand, with arms crossed in the traditional style. With Gwen's long skirt flowing out behind, they swooped gracefully from side to side, round and round in the firelight.

A ring of straw with some planks laid on it had been spread at a little distance from the fire, and as we tired, we could sit down and warm ourselves. Somebody had brought a half sack of potatoes, and before the fire had been lit these had been tucked in around the base of the bonfire on top of the soil. About an hour later they were raked out, coated with thick, crackly black skin. When this was broken open, the fragrant hot potato, floury and steaming, smelled and tasted delicious in the cold air. Lard pails of tea, with cream and sugar added, had been set into the red hot embers, and the boiling tea was poured into enamel cups and passed around.

By this time puddles of water were beginning to form on top of the ice around the fire, and

spreading out towards our feet. The fire was
dying down, and the burning embers were
collapsing into the water. We gathered ourselves
together, Father unscrewed the skates from my
boots, unstrapped Betty's and slung them over his
shoulder. Then shouting goodbyes, the merry party
in sleighs or buggies, on horseback or walking,
set out in different directions to their homesteads.

The last sparks of the bonfire died down, and
under that vast scintillating dome, the crisp
silence of the frosty winter night returned to
the little lake.

Prairie Fire

A little fire is quickly trodden out
Which, being suffered, rivers cannot quench.
Shakespeare: Henry VI Part 3 Act 4

One Saturday in the early fall, Betty, Tommy
and I were alone on the farm. Mother and Father
had driven into Strathmore for supplies, taking
the twins with them, and the current farm help
had taken the weekend off and gone up to Calgary.
It had been a very hot dry season, and in the
early afternoon I sat in the shade on the front
steps with a book on my lap. Beyond the farmyard
and cow pasture I could see the fine field of
wheat that sloped up towards the fenced section
line on the eastern half of the farm, and beyond
that stretched many miles of open grassland, the
prairie grass now tinder dry.

The wheat was ripe, ready for the binder, and
the heavy, pale gold heads stood up thick and
straight on the dry, brittle stalks. It was a
beautiful sight, the best crop we had had of the
new Red Fife, the seed for which had been
provided by the C.P.R. Experimental Farm, and
which hopefully was to produce many bushels of
fine pedigreed seed, to be sold to the farmers in
the district.

If the weather held, the cutting was to start
on Monday morning, and the men would be out in
the field at daybreak. The binder and four horse
team would work from corner to corner of the
forty acre field, gradually drawing into the
centre, and the sheaves, firmly tied with the
strong bindertwine, would drop from the binder in
rows, on the stiff, dry stubble, to be gathered
up and built into stooks.

Before the combine was invented, good
stooking was an important part of grain farming,
and the stooker, arms well protected with long
sleeves, and hands covered with thick leather
gloves, would gather up two sheaves, one under

each arm with the heads facing forward, choose a level spot, then plunk the sheaves down firmly on the stubble, lean the tops together, then add two more sheaves on the opposite sides. Four more would be leaned against the first four, making a stook that would stand against a strong wind. Woe betide the stooker who worked with bearded wheat or barley without arms and hands well covered. His skin would be scratched, red and prickly for days afterwards.

It had been very still and quiet as I sat on the steps that afternoon, but there was a softness in the air, a faint suggestion of coming change, a sense of waiting, and a feeling that all nature was pausing briefly, in preparation for what was to come, the fall and then winter. A little gust of wind, hot and dry, touched my cheek and I looked up and over towards the wheat field. I could see the heads bowing stiffly as a rising wind riffled across the field. Suddenly I had a feeling that something was wrong, something alarming was happening, and I scrabbled to my feet, realizing at the same moment that I had caught a faint whiff of smoke, of burning grass.

The year before we had had a frightening experience when a prairie fire, whipped by a strong wind, had come very close to the farm buildings. It had started in a fenced pasture across the road allowance from Radfords, perhaps a quarter of a mile from the house. In minutes after the first little spiral of smoke curled up from the dry grass, the flames were shooting ten to twenty feet into the air, and the spreading line of fire was racing towards us, the gusting wind blowing tufts of burning grass far ahead of the flames, each to start a fresh blaze. Luckily there was a small, deep slough in the near corner of the field, in the path of the fire, which together with the road allowance slowed the blaze, so that the fire fighters with wet sacks that they had dipped in the slough, were able to beat out the fire. In that case we were fortunate that the farm hand and Father were at home and that the water from the slough was immediately available.

But now, on this Saturday morning, there was nobody at home but my two sisters and myself. It was about the year 1915, Betty would be eleven years old, Tommy nine and I thirteen. The wind was coming from the south east land, so the smell of burning grass must be coming from that direction, from the open grassland beyond the wheat field, but as yet I could see nothing. The land sloped away slightly from the top of the field, so that a fire, if there were one, could be out of sight.

I shouted, and Betty and Tommy came out of the barn. I waved to them and they ran up towards the house, and now the smell of burning grass wafted on the wind was stronger. We all remembered the prairie fire of the year before and realized the danger of a fire starting over the rise to the east, and probably coming towards the wheat field. We knew how the other fire had been fought, the flames beaten down with wet sacks. We had plenty of sacks in the granary but there would be no water up there on the dry grassland. Suddenly we saw a spurt of sulphur coloured smoke puff up from beyond the rise and streak out across the skyline.

"If it's a prairie fire it could burn up our wheat! We'll have to go up and fight it with wet sacks," Betty stopped, realizing as I had, that we would need water, and that there would be none out there on the high ground. "The democrat , we could put the rain barrel in the back, pump some water into it! We could drive up there and save the wheat!" Betty's quick mind ticked over like a modern computer, popping out the answer to each problem.

"Lucy's in the barn, I'll harness her!" Tommy's apple cheeks were rosy with excitement as she raced off down to the horse barn. Betty and I pulled the light democrat up to the pump, rolled the empty rain barrel over to it and with much levering and pushing we managed to heave it up onto the back of the cart.

The democrat was a useful pre-truck vehicle on the ranches and farms, a sort of light dray, with two removable double seats, which could be lifted off and the cart used to carry sacks of potatoes and flour, crates of chickens and cartons of groceries. With the two comfortable seats firmly clamped onto the sides, it could take the whole family to Church on Sundays, or to a family picnic.

We pumped water into the buckets, carried them to the back of the democrat, and emptied them into the barrel. Tommy was backing Lucy between the shafts and fastening the traces, and we threw armsful of sacks onto the democrat, pushing some into the barrel to soak. We climbed in, Betty drove, and Tommy and I stood on either side of the barrel, struggling to hold it from tipping over, as we bounced over gopher holes and ruts. The section was fenced, and so we had to drive out the front gate and up the road allowance to the east corner.

Betty used the whip on poor old Lucy, who being retired from heavy work, was not used to being hurried, but she broke into a stumbling trot. By the time we reached the upper corner of the wheat field, we could see the smoke blowing towards us, and as we topped the rise we could see the fire itself, about a hundred yards or so down the slope. It had not yet spread very far, but the line was widening at both ends, and it was sweeping fairly fast towards us and the wheat field.

Now we saw something else, some distance away to the left and beyond the fire was a hayrack and team with a small figure holding the horses' heads. Two men were running towards the fire and as we watched they started trying to beat it out with hayforks. I recognized them, John and Arthur Fitch, brothers who homesteaded on adjoining farms some miles to the east of Radfords, and James, the son of Arthur, who was the boy holding the horses.

We found out later they had been carting hay
from their haystacks, where the hay had been cut
earlier in the year, to their barns, when they
caught sight of the fire. We knew them well and
James, then about ten years old, helped herd
their stock and rode over to Radfords from time
to time on a cayuse pony. He was the youngest of
four brothers, the eldest of whom had enlisted in
the Canadian Forces, the Great War then being in
its second year. He was later reported missing
and then later still, as killed in action.

We tied Lucy, who was snorting and showing
signs of alarm, to a fencepost, and started
pulling the sacks out of the barrel, and then ran
down towards the fire with them in our arms. The
men, who were not having much success with the
hayforks, shouted when they saw what we were
carrying, dropped their forks and grabbed the
dripping sacks.

We were not to be outdone in this exciting
derring-do, and stamped and flailed and shouted
as enthusiastically as the men. Fortunately, on
that day the wind, which had risen so suddenly,
was not gusty enough to whip the flames to
dangerous proportions, and it slackened to a
breeze as we fought the blaze.

Some time later the danger was over, and the
fire out, although here and there on the acre or
two of blackened grass, small diminishing wisps
of smoke still spiralled upwards. Tired, hot and
very dirty, the two men, ourselves and Jamie, who
had driven the hayrack up to the fence and tied
the team beside Lucy, sat on the ground and wiped
our faces with the remains of a damp sack. My
cotton print dress was badly scorched and torn,
Betty's curly hair and eyebrows were singed, and
our faces were streaked with perspiration and
ash.

"That was a sensible thing you girls did
today, bringing up the sacks and water barrel. We
might have had a hard time killing that blaze
with the hayforks." John Fitch smiled at us, his
grizzled hair standing on end and his face red

and shining with sweat. "Was your Dad away?" We explained that we were alone on the farm as our parents had gone to town for spare parts for the binder, harvest supplies and bindertwine.

"When he gets back better tell him to send somebody up here this evening to keep an eye on the fire. If the wind strengthens it just might blaze up again."

That day, for the first time, I think I felt the joy of feeling important, of having accomplished, or at least, having helped accomplish something worthwhile. We were enormously proud of ourselves and probably took most of the credit for dowsing the fire.

Poor Father, after his long day in town, spent most of that night sitting alone out on the prairie, under the golden harvest moon, keeping an eye on the remains of that prairie fire.

Prairie Legends

"From Goulies and ghosties
And long-legged beasties
And things that go bump in the night
Good Lord, deliver us!
Old Cornish Prayer

There was a fascinating legend in the early years of this century. The story was that at a certain lonely spot in central Alberta, where a shallow coulee runs down into a small, sedgy lake, strange sounds could be heard at the dark of the moon. Two shepherds camping nearby had heard the sound of many hooves and the grunting and shuffling of a herd of large animals passing down the coulee to the lake. Knowing that there were no range cattle in that vicinity they were surprised. In the morning when they looked for signs of the herd, they were amazed to find that not a blade of grass had been disturbed, and not a single hoofmark could be seen in the soft muddy shore of the lake. Several times after that others reported the same eerie experience in the same area. What better foundation for a good ghost story than the wiping out in one lifetime of the great herds of buffalo that had roamed the prairies for countless centuries!

According to the records of the Hudson's Bay Company, the first white man to have seen the American Bison, and named it after the East Indian buffalo, was Henry Kelsey. He was a remarkable young man, who came out from England in 1683 to the Hudson's Bay Company post at Fort Nelson, later known as York Factory, on the western shore of the Hudson's Bay. He did not like the stern discipline of the Governor and ran away, joining a tribe of Stone, or Stoney Indians. He spent two years with them, learning their language and ways. He eventually returned to the Fort, and because of his experiences with the Indians, he was very valuable to the Company, which then sent him on several exploratory expeditions.

On his first trip to the north he saw musk oxen,which he described as "ill-shapen beasts, their body being bigger than an ox." Later he penetrated west,as far as the Saskatchewan River and saw the great herds of prairie buffalo. One can picture him climbing a long, gradual slope of rolling prairie, breasting the ridge and creeping forward, to reconnoitre for signs of unfriendly Indians. An enormous vista opens up before him as he looks out over the breathtaking stretch of country. Perhaps fifty miles away, in the blue distance, the crest of the next ridge is silhouetted against the horizon. Imagine his feelings, as he sees, spread out across the immense valley, the restless brown carpet of animals, great shaggy headed bulls, sleek cows, and leggy calves.

Stories of the fantastic migrations, when the closely packed beasts covered the ground as far as the eye could see, and took days to pass a given spot,were still being told by eye witnesses at the turn of the century. But the slaughter of the great animals by the Indians and the early white immigrants, had been so relentless and ruthless, that at that time not one wild buffalo roamed the prairies. A few small bands of wood buffalo were reported in the Peace River Country.

When the extinction of the prairie buffalo seemed inevitable, with only a very few animals existing, in a small herd owned by two Montana ranchers, the Canadian Government purchased some of these tamed animals, and shipped them to the Elk Island Park, near Edmonton, to found the herd that became one of Alberta's greatest tourist attractions.

In 1910 it was still possible to find relics of the wild buffalo that had disappeared from the ranges so quickly. Their enormously thick skulls with the stubby up-curved horns resisted decay, long after the rest of the skeleton had crumbled to dust, and could occasionally be picked up around the sloughs. Ranchers and homesteaders nailed them on their barn doors, and on corral gates, chalk white ghostly mementoes of what had been an inevitable tragedy.

In days when transportation depended on horse drawn buggies and sleighs, most men who had to do winter driving, owned a buffalo coat. The livery barns also rented them out with their sleighs and teams. The shaggy, coarse red brown hair was almost indestructible, and excellent insulation against the bitter winds. Doctors who drove miles in open cutters, through blizzards and in sub-zero temperatures, owed their lives on many occasions, to the great coats that covered them from head to foot. Most families owned buffalo robes to tuck over knees in buggies, sleighs and cutters.

A couple of miles southeast of Radfords, was a slough, that appeared to have been considerably larger at one time. Well above the high water mark, was a second well defined line circling the slough. The smooth slope between the present water level, and the older higher water line, must have been the muddy shore of the slough at one time. It was pitted with shallow, oval depressions, each about twelve feet long, by six wide, and about two feet deep. The ground was firm, and the depressions smooth, and all identical in shape. These were buffalo wallows.One of the last small herds to have ranged there must have watered at the slough, wallowing in the soft mud, as was their habit, to relieve themselves of the swarming deerflies and mosquitoes. Probably the following summers were dry seasons, and in the drought the slough receded,the wallows baking hard in the shape left by the bodies of the great beasts. As spring rains came, the grass gradually grew over the wallows and helped preserve them. The thick, tangled, and deep growing roots of the prairie "moss", would solidify the sandy soil, and hold the shape of the wallows during the future wet seasons.

It was a wonderful place for children to play. A flock of sheep was herded over the range at that time, and they kept the grass cropped short. In spring the aromatic fragrance of wild peppermint and sweetgrass rose into the warm air, patches of pink and magenta shooting stars made bright washes of colour against the pale green grass, and the frogs kept up a throaty chorus at night. Red winged blackbirds hung their woven nests in the tall reeds at the shallow end of the slough, and rose in chirring clouds if any intruder went too close. In the longer grass around the water edge, ducks nested, and little flotillas of ducklings sailed in the placid water.

Early in this century, there lived in a log cabin on the Serviceberry Creek, a couple of ancient bachelor brothers who had rounded up the wild horses in the foothills, corraled and then broke them for the cowboys. They told fascinating stories of the days when they had freighted across the plains, with the creaking Red River carts, days when the buffalo was making his last gallant stand for his right to the prairie ranges. They were gone before our time, but they and their stories had become legends. We could picture them sitting around the red hot stoves of farm kitchens and country stores in winter time, as they explained the riddle of the wallows, and told again and again the story of the phantom herd, that was said to move on dark nights down the coulee to the lake. Some listeners scoffed of course, and suggested solutions to the mystery, the high wind soughing through the fragrant wolfbroom and scrub poplar, possibly the grumble of distant thunder, or the whirring flight of night birds, but those who claimed they had actually heard the strange noises in the night, merely shook their heads and had no explanation to offer.

Father drove home from Strathmore in the dusk one evening in early spring, came into the kitchen, took off his sheepskin, then sat down to the plate of supper Mother had kept warm in the oven. He seemed unusually thoughtful, and after a while

Mother asked him if he were worried about something. Father patted his mustache with his serviette.

"Well, not worried," he replied, "but a bit mystified." Betty and I, who were doing our homework at the other end of the table and were glad of an excuse to drop our pencils, pricked up our ears. Father told us, that as he had been driving along a lonely part of the road allowance a couple of miles from town, he had caught sight out of the corner of his eye, of something moving on the other side of the barbwire fence. He had had the impression of a horse and rider, a large white horse and what he thought was an Indian from the way he was riding, seemingly bareback, legs hanging down and toes turned in. All this was sort of a fleeting impression as when he turned his head the vision disappeared, and by the time he was looking squarely in its direction, there was nothing there. We realized from his voice, that for once Father was quite serious, and not pulling one of his practical jokes on us. He went on to tell us that he had wondered if he had fallen asleep and was dreaming, but when he drove on, he saw again, out of the corner of his eye, the tall horse and rider, silently keeping pace with the team and buggy. He drove on for a couple of minutes, still conscious of the thing moving on the other side of the fence, then quickly turned his head and caught a clear picture of the white horse, and what he was sure was an Indian riding it, but as he stared at it, it seemed to dissolve into the deepening dusk, and there was nothing there but the prairie landscape.

In those days there were many hair raising story books for children, of ghosts, witches, hobgoblins and poltergeists. We were well supplied with them from Grandfather Pardon's London Publishing House, and I read all I could get my hands on. As Father told of his strange experience, I could feel the hair prickling on the back of my neck. A real ghost story!

Mother leaned her chin on the palm of her hand, "Harry, were you in the King Edward before you left town?"

"Yes, E., and I had one with Walter Harvey. We were discussing putting on hail insurance this year. But it was only one." He held up his first finger. "And I was perfectly sober when I started home."

And so we had our own ghost story, and from then on, I never passed along that piece of the road without keeping my eyes open for the white horse and Indian rider, and hoping with a shiver, that I might catch sight of them.

Hailstorm

Here we are! Here we are! Here we are again!
There's Pat and Mac and Tommy and Jack and
                            Joe
When there's trouble brewing
When there's something doing
Are we downhearted?
No! Let 'em all come!
Here we are! Here we are again!

From "Storm and Stress" by Charles Knight
                                    (1775)

Harry Petter was not a remittance man, but he did have some of the finer characteristics of those ne'er-do-well younger sons of wealthy families, who were being shipped out to Canada around the turn of the century, in the hope they would make something out of themselves. Father enjoyed his scotch and soda but never drank to excess, and he received no remittances from home, as his father had died four years before he emigrated to Canada. However, he had a happy-go-lucky temperament, a cheerful Mr.Micawber-like faith that when times were difficult "something would turn up", that inevitably all would be well in the end.

He had an amazing resiliency. He would come in exhausted and taut with strain after some disastrous happening, a stillborn calf, the chickenhouse raided by hungry coyotes, the first load of new wheat graded 3 instead of 1 hard at the elevator, but after a short rest and a cup of tea he would pick himself up and cry, "Are we downhearted?" and we would all shout cheerfully "No".

Father had a never failing sense of humour and could throw care aside at a moment's notice. He made many friends amongst the ranchers and farmers in the area, and would help any neighbour in need when the occasion called. He never blamed others for his mistakes and seldom showed sign of discouragement or worry. But Mother worried! Owing money to the grocer was a shocking disgrace, and she was humiliated if the bill couldn't be paid promptly at the end of the month.

Harry Petter must have inherited some intuitive skill from his inventive father and grandfather, which enabled him to repair farm machinery with extra-ordinary ingenuity. In the middle of harvest when the reaper broke down and time was of the essence, he would mend it with bindertwine or a piece of wire. A rusty nail or a screw would repair a plough or hayrake at a time when a lost day's work in the field could be disastrous.

In the spring of 1915, Father, having been turned down at the recruiting office in Calgary, had decided the best thing he could do to help the war effort would be to grow wheat, lots of wheat, and of the best quality. He was advised to sow pedigreed seed. Red Fife and Marquis were the finest wheats available at that time, before the ruinous red rust to which they were very susceptible, spread across the grain fields of the west.

By early summer the fields of wheat promised well, and when headed out the stretches of shimmering green, waving in the warm winds as sun and cloud shadow swept over them, were a beautiful sight. By the middle of August the wheat was ripening, the heavy heads on thick strong stalks now golden in the strong, hot sunshine.

The weather grew hotter, and one morning there was an ominous stillness, a closeness that was oppressive. The birds disappeared, and the animals stood listlessly in the pastures. Over us the sky seemed cloudless, but the blue had disappeared and a strange coppery film dimmed the sun. Away to the northwest we could see thunderheads building up over the horizon, and during the afternoon they slowly grew closer. The heat seemed to press down on us, everything was so still.

Father had gone to Strathmore that morning on some business, and Ted Maitland, the current farmhand was cutting hay a couple of miles away to the north. About mid afternoon we saw him coming down the road allowance with his team. Mother went out to meet him.

"Looks like a bad one, thought I had better get back before it hits us." He wiped the perspiration from his face. "Could you send one of the girls out for the cows? I'll get the horses in and round up the calves in the pasture."

Betty was sent off, riding bareback on Nitchie, the Cayuse pony, to bring in the milk cows, and I was told to try and get the geese and turkeys into the chicken house. The cloud masses were moving closer now, travelling low over the prairie, and we could see them boiling up and down like bubbles on a pot of soup. Underneath they were blue-black but the tops were silvery white, and they were moving faster now towards us. Betty was coming down the road with the milk cows and Mother ran down to open the gate to let them in.

"It looks like hail, go in and get a couple of pillows up against the big window in the bedroom," she shouted at me, holding up her long skirt as she ran, "and take the children in with you."

I knew what to do, as previous hailstorms had broken windows in other homes. We had been advised that holding pillows against a window might prevent the shattering of the glass, when the wind and hailstones hit it. Our big window facing the north west would now take the brunt of what was approaching. I hustled Tommy and the twins inside, then Tommy and I ran upstairs and managed to pull a dressing table in front of the window, stuffing the pillows from the bed between it and the glass. Then I ran outside again to see what was happening. As I looked towards the fast approaching storm I felt a sudden chill breath of air on my face, and saw that there was a solid grey wall coming straight towards us. I could hear a dull roar, and saw a couple of flashes of lightning, followed by the rumble of thunder. I looked down towards the stable, and saw Mother and Betty herding the last of the cows into the barn, then pulling the big door shut behind them. I ran back into the house and slammed the door.

The wind struck the house like a solid thing. It had turned very dark, and the lightning flashes lit up the house. Then came a sudden crash as the hail hit us. The twins, Tommy and I, huddled together, too frightened to speak, and listened to the uproar outside. In time the noise gradually lessened, the gusts of wind came less frequently, and then suddenly, unbelievably, the sun burst through the clouds, and shone on a world of sparkling ice. The hail must have been a couple of inches thick, but it was already melting and steam was rising from the ground.

As the storm cleared, Mother, Betty and Ted, came up from the barn, sloshing through the melting hailstones, and we met them at the kitchen door. There seemed to be no damage to the house and no broken windows. The animals were safe, but everything in the vegetable garden, which we could see from the kitchen windows, seemed to be flattened under a sheet of gleaming ice. Mother sat down, wiped her face with a towel, and unlaced her wet boots. The hem of her long skirt was soaking wet.

Father arrived shortly afterwards. We were so thankful to see him, but seeing the expression on his face as he came throught the door, we looked anxiously at him, and each other, and nobody said a word. He came slowly into the kitchen, hung his hat on the hook behind the door, and stood for a moment looking across the room at Mother, then walked over to the table and sat down.

"All gone, Edith! Hardly a stalk left, all the wheat beaten into the ground." He leaned his head on his hand, looking more shaken and discouraged than I had ever seen him. Betty and I looked at each other in consternation, Tommy was

frowning fiercely, and the twins stood by the
table staring up at Father with woebegone faces.
For Father to be so obviously shattered, was
unbelievable, he usually took the brunt of crises
and disasters, with a calm unflappable fortitude,
a quiet assurance, that no matter what the
trouble, everything would turn out all right in
the long run. Now he looked so disheartened that
we realized that this was a worse than usual
calamity. Also, we had some personal interest in
the loss of the wheat crop, Betty and I had spent
many hours earlier in the year tip-toeing
carefully up and down the rows of flourishing
wheat, pulling out the odd spike of mustard,
shepherd's purse or sowthistle.

Father told us that the storm had cut only a
narrow swath across the land from northwest to
southeast, that Radfords had been directly in its
path, and that he had seen the storm ahead of
him, as he drove over the rise on his way back
from Strathmore. When he had reached the road
allowance that skirted the wheat field, he had
seen the havoc the storm had wreaked. Mother
walked over to the table and sat down opposite
him. She leaned over and put her hand on his.

"Cheer up, Harry. It could be worse. Ted got
the calves and horses in, Betty fetched the cows.
We got the geese and turkeys under cover, and no
windows broken. It's a big loss, but we'll manage.
Don't worry." She got up, went over to the
cookstove and shook out the ashes, put newspaper
and kindling into the firebox and set a match to
it, filled the kettle and put it on. As always, a
good strong cup of tea was Mother's surest worry
antidote and comfort, in times of trouble such as
this.

Ted had taken off his heavy boots and was
standing in his socks near the window, listening
to Father and Mother. As the kettle started to
sing he went over to the cookstove, spooned tea
into the teapot and poured on the boiling water,
then patted the teacosy down on the teapot. As
they drank hot tea our parents and Ted talked

about the storm which had passed over so quickly,
the violent wind and hail, then discussed what
should be done about the churned-up wheat field
when the ground dried.The wheat would be ploughed
in for summerfallow, and would provide good com-
post for the next year's crop.

Father's face slowly brightened, and he
straightened up his shoulders. Mother smiled, the
sun shone brilliantly; Ted emptied the teapot
into the slop pail and piled the teacups. The
rest of us cheered up. Suddenly Father pushed his
chair back, stood up and shouted his usual,

"Cheer up everybody! Are we downhearted?" and
dutifully as always, we all shouted back "NO!"

In later years the farmers were able to take
out hail insurance on their crops, and although
much damage was done almost every year in
scattered areas from the fierce storms, the
losses were at least partially covered.

Our Animals

"All animals are equal, but
some are more equal than others."

George Orwell - Animal Farm

In the old Radfords home, near Dawlish in the beautiful Devonshire countryside, the Pardon family had lived for several generations. The house stood in a large garden, surrounded by fields and an apple orchard, and in the spring-time, the ground under the ancient twisted apple trees was sprinkled with great clumps of daffo-odils. Beyond the fields the rolling heath rose towards the high red cliffs that looked out over the English Channel.

Mary and John Pardon, our Grandparents, lived most of their lives at Radfords, and raised three daughters and three sons there. The children had many pets during their childhood years, ponies, a donkey, cats and dogs, and even a goat, and they all learned to ride and handle horses.

So Mother faced with the new life in Alberta, knew a good deal about the handling of the farm animals. She was convinced that no domestic creature would deliberately harm a child unless it was frightened or attacked, and we were taught to be gentle and quiet with all our farm animals. In all the years at Radford, I have no recollect-ion of one of us being kicked or hurt by a horse, or other animal. With the exception perhaps of an angry bull, we were never frightened of them, and we all played freely in the barns and corrals, and out in the fields, riding bareback both the horses and cows. When one of us was sent out to bring in the milk cows, we would ride one of them back to the cowbarn.

We had an original method of getting up on a cow, or unsaddled horse, when out on the prairie, if there was no one handy to give us a leg up. If we could not manoeuvre the animal up to a fence, or beside the large mound of excavated earth beside a badger hole, we would stand beside its head until it was quietly cropping grass, then quickly and gently slip one leg over its neck. Then, as it threw its head up, slide onto its back. This worked most of the time, particularly with a horse, because a mane to hang on to was a great help, but sometimes the scheme misfired, and we would slip off and find ourselves rolling on the grass.There were inevitable falls, sometimes when an animal stumbled into a gopher hole or shied, but we soon learned the best way to land, to roll ourselves up with arms and head turned in, and legs drawn up, and to hit the ground as nearly like a ball as possible, so that one rolled rather than crashed.

When bringing in the milk cows from pasture, we would round them up and head them towards home, then walk beside one, usually gentle old Biddy, until she lowered her head to snatch a mouthful of grass, then we would seize the opportunity to be swung easily up onto her back. Then with a little gentle prodding, the cow would amble slowly on towards the milk barn with the others meekly falling into line behind.

Biddy was the bell-wether of our milk cows, a big craggy cow, mottled red and white, with small curved up horns. She produced a fine calf every spring, and gave bucketsful of creamy milk. Some warm sunny days I would pretend I was a cowherd, and would spend hours sitting out on the quiet prairie amongst the browsing cows. After a while I would roll over and lie face down in the scented grass, the soft wind blowing over me, and the sun warm on my back. Presently Biddy would become a little concerned or perhaps just curious, probably wondering what I was up to. I would lie perfectly still, and eventually I would hear her drawing slowly nearer, tearing steadily at the tough grass as she approached. Presently she would be standing over me, I would feel her great rubbery nose moving over the back of my neck and

and head, as she blew her fragrant breath through my hair. Then I would roll over, throw my arms round her great neck, and rub behind her large floppy ears. She would stand quietly, head stretched out and eyes closed, and start slowly chewing her cud.

Nick and Fatty were a team of light weight work horses, so totally unlike each other in colour, shape and disposition, that it was a mystery that they were sold to Father as a team. Nick was a tall, handsome horse, shiny black with a white star and four well feathered fetlocks. He had a sweet disposition, was very gentle with us, and we rode him a good deal, usually bareback, but sometimes with his harness on, as we took him back and forth to the work fields. He had a kindly sense of humour, and would often prance a little with one of us on his back, but when he felt he had been ridden enough, he would slowly bend his front knees, fold his back legs under, then collapse over on his side and commence to roll. Whoever was on his back, had to scrabble away on hands and knees to safety. Once I had ridden him some distance, and he no doubt had had more than enough of me. It was very hot, and the horseflies and mosquitoes were particularly trying. We were passing along the edge of one of the shallow, weedy little sloughs in the big pasture, Nick's big hooves squelching into the soft, alkaline mud. Suddenly he did his "had enough of this" gambit, went down on his knees into the mud and gradually sank onto his side, with me frantically struggling in the slime and muddy sludge to safety. I'll swear he had a satisfied smirk on his big black face. We were both covered with mud and I felt sure he was laughing at me. After I cleaned up, and Nick dried off, Father made me curry him until he was clean, and his coat sleek and shiny again, which of course he enjoyed.

Fatty was a faded, light bay with a white star and one white fetlock, but he was an ugly, craggy horse, slightly swayback, his joints bumpy, and mis-shaped. He had probably been starved and ill treated in his colt-hood years, and so understandably mistrusted all humans. On the slightest provocation he would flatten his ears, show the whites of his eyes, and bare his long yellow teeth. No creature can look more evil and dangerous than an angry horse. But Fatty's looks were deceptive, and he never harmed one of us. He would grab a sleeve or coat tail and shake us, but we were not afraid of him, and this no doubt had something to do with his tolerance of children.

He was loose in the corral one winter's day, when one of the men went in with a halter to catch him, leaving the gate open. Fatty saw the halter and the open gate at the same time, kicked up his heels, flattened his ears, and headed for the gate at a gallop. Me Too, about four years old and so bundled up against the cold that she couldn't run, happened to be standing in the gateway, and right in Fatty's way. He gathered his hooves together, and leaped right over her head, just as Mother came running down from the house. Me Too had fallen flat on her face, the hired man stood white and shaken, but nobody was hurt, as Fatty headed happily for the big pasture.

The home pasture was a fenced area of about five acres, with a wooden gate between it and the corral, behind the horse barn. Our purebread Clydesdale stallion, Sonsie, was often turned out into this pasture and he would prance and paw the turf, throwing his handsome head up and shaking his heavy, flowing mane. Then he would roll luxuriously on the close cropped, springy turf. He was ordinarily very gentle and good natured, except in spring time when the mares were in heat, and another male horse was nearby.

One sunny, windy spring morning Sonsie, was out in the pasture. Small drifts of dirty melting snow lay in the shady spots, but patches of blue and purple crocuses were already pushing their way throught the drying grass. Meadowlarks were singing cheerfully, and red winged blackbirds swooped around the reedy sloughs.

I was up in the hayloft, on this blue and gold spring morning, when I suddenly heard a great commotion somewhere behind the barn, shouting, thundering hooves, stamping, snorting, and shrill squealing. I scrambled down the ladder and rushed out to the corral, to see what all the fuss was about. On the far side of the pasture Sonsie was chasing our beloved horse Nick! Ears back, teeth bared, he was slashing out viciously with his wicked front hooves. Standing in the gateway to the pasture, shouting and waving his arms, was Rawlins, the stableman. He had absent mindedly turned Nick out into the pasture, apparently not realizing, that in springtime, another male horse might turn a gentle, peaceful stallion into a raging maniac.

I take no credit to myself for any kind of bravery. I had not the slightest fear of Sonsie, nor any sense of danger to myself, and have no intention of trying to make myself out a brave heroine, rushing into mortal danger to save our dear Nick. I had not a doubt in the world that I could control that powerful animal. The stallion had driven Nick into a corner of the field, against the wire, and I knew what barbed wire could do to a heavy animal if it crashed into it. Rawlins was holding the gate, ready to slam it shut if the horses came near him, but I pushed past him and ran out across the grass shouting "Stop it! Stop it! Sonsie, stop it!"

Behind me Rawlins was screaming "You crazy kid, come back! You'll be killed! Look out, they're coming this way! Oh God!" and I could hear him crash the gate shut.

I kept shouting as I ran, and Sonsie seemed to hesitate. He turned his head towards me, then slowed down, no doubt confused by this interruption, and for the moment, I had taken his attention from the other horse. I ran up to him and caught his halter, scolding him. He shook his head, the spume flying from his muzzle, panting with all that ferocious effort. Nick meantime had seized his opportunity, and galloped on towards the gate, Rawlins opened it, and let him through into the safety of the horse corral. I stroked Sonsie's velvety nose and rubbed behind his ears, telling him he was a very bad boy to attack poor Nick. He lowered his head and rubbed his face against my coat, for all the world as if he was saying he was sorry. It was all over and apparently nobody any the worse. I walked back to the gate, where Rawlins still stood safely on the far side, his face expressionless. He opened the gate to let me through without a word, and I went over to Nick who was standing panting near the stable door. Apart from a few scratches on his side from the barbed wire, he was not harmed.

It is my conviction, that it is part of the law of survival for an animal to sense fear in another creature, animal or human, and to recognize its power over anything fearful of it. A small creature might well be able to control an animal much larger that itself, by being totally unconscious of danger from it. A small dog, for instance, herding cattle, each animal many times the size of the dog, and capable of trampling the dog to death, but the dog is in complete control of the entire herd. The dog and the cattle instinctively know it, the cattle fearful, and the dog fearless. No matter how well one might disguise one's inward fear, an animal senses it. A nervous rider can never be in complete control of his horse. If I had gone into that pasture on that long ago day inwardly frightened, if outwardly fearless, I doubt if Sonsie would have paid any attention to me, and would probably have battered Nick to pieces against the cruel barbed wire, and no telling what he might have done to me.

I have another vivid memory of a strange happening in that horse pasture. It must have been within a year or two or our arrival at Radfords, when I was eight or nine years old. I went out behind the barn one moonlight night and although it was early evening, the sun had

long since set. I never had the slightest fear of
the dark,and was often out alone on the exciting,
mysterious prairie. This night, for some reason,
I went out of the big door at the back of the
barn, through the corral to the gate into the
pasture, and stood there in the bright light of
the full moon. Three or four horses were standing
quietly in a corner of the corral. It was very
still and silent, a magic night, but suddenly a
most extraordinary, and literally hair raising
sound filled the night, a high pitched, wavering
noise that seemed to swirl around me. I couldn't
tell from which direction it was coming. I was
too startled to run, and grabbed the gate rail to
steady myself.The sound was so unearthly- ghosts?
witches? goblins? All kinds of horrors raced
through my head. The sound gradually lessened and
seemed to recede to a distance, and then it rose
again to a new crescendo, but again I couldn't
tell from where it was coming. Suddenly a burst
of furious, deep throated barking came from the
barnyard as Brindle, our Great Dane, voiced his
indignation and alarm at the disturbance. The
weird, unearthly noise ceased immediately, as if
somebody had pulled a switch. Completely bewildered, I stared out across the field, and was just
in time to see a shadowy line of small, vague
shapes fade down the slope of the little hill at
the far end of the pasture and quietly disappear.
Coyotes! Of course! Baying the moon. As the truth
dawned on me, my heart started beating again. I
could breathe and my limbs gradually unfroze. But
now the farm yard had come to life, there was a
great commotion and clucking in the henhouse, the
horses were milling around, stamping and throwing
up their heads in alarm, and I could hear inquir-
ing grunts coming from the pigsties. I had heard
about this little wolf's strange habit of high
pitched wailing at the full moon, and had read
about it in stories of the west, but I did not
know about the ghostly ventriloquistic way they
could throw the sound in all directions. To
confuse their enemies, no doubt!

When my knees had stopped shaking, I walked slowly back towards the farmyard, puzzling about the strange experience. The animals had quietened, but as I came through the dark barn, and out again into the moonlight, I saw Brindle standing halfway up to the house. He was staring out towards the little hill, and pointing like a hunting dog, with his tail standing out in a straight line. I called to him and he turned to me, then came over and rubbed his big head against my arm obviously trying to reassure me.

Strangely, I have no recollection of ever again hearing the coyote chorus as I did that night. The prairie wolf is a small furtive animal, more like a fox, and not as large or dangerous as the timber wolf, but they are clever little animals, seldom seen in daylight. In 1910 there were many coyotes in Alberta, and they raided the chicken runs, killed lambs and calves, and so were shot and trapped almost to extinction. As the colonists took over their habitat, those coyotes that survived, moved farther and farther north to safety.

Our Pigs

"This little pig went to market,
This little pig stayed home,
This little big had roast beef,
This little pig had none,
And this little pig cried Wee,Wee,Wee!
I can't find my way home."
Tommy Thumb's Little Story Book (1760)

Times were particularly hard one year. Crops had been poor, the spring and summer had been dry, early frosts had done a lot of damage, and the price of wheat had dropped. So that winter Father decided that the following spring he would raise pigs for the market.

We had a huge Yorkshire sow that we had christened Martha, and she was one of our family pets. She roamed all over the farm, and when Father was ploughing with team and hand plough, she would follow him up and down the field, plodding along in the furrow until she was tired out, when she would roll over onto the soft fresh soil, and rest until Father came round on the next lap. Then she would heave herself up and drop back into the furrow and follow him again, grunting gently. She raised many large litters of piglets in her lifetime, annd the twins would pretend to milk her. She would stand patiently while they pummeled away at her tiny teats. Sometimes they would even ride about the farmyard on her back, one behind the other.

Sometime later, Father acquired a huge black Berkshire boar, from an English farmer by the name of Walter Harvey, and because Mr. Harvey was a large dark man with a lot of black hair and bushy black beard, we girls innocently named the boar Walter. Some time afterwards, Mr. Harvey happened to drop in and stayed for lunch. Looking round the table at the five of us he asked how the boar was settling down. No doubt our parents were embarrassed to hear us cheerfully assure Mr.

Harvey that "Walter" was doing well, liked his
sty, and was getting along with Martha beautifully.

Mr. Harvey must have been a kindly and under-
standing man, he had three children of his own,
and I remember that after a brief silence during
which he glanced calmly at us with a completely
expressionless face, he turned quietly to Mother
and started a discussion on something or other,
no doubt with the considerate intent of reassur-
ing our parents, that he understood the ways of
children and had taken no umbrage.

Next Father bought a couple of Durocs, smaller
pigs than our large white Yorkshire and black
Berkshire, and rusty red in colour. The result
was that before long we had a fine herd of medium
sized pigs, spotted black, white and red. They
flourished, and after the wheat crop was harvest-
ed they were turned out in the stubble, and fended
for themselves. Father had been up to Calgary and
had made a good deal with Kolb's Restaurant, one
of the largest in Calgary at that time. He was to
ship up two dressed porkers each week throughout
the winter.

Shortly after this, probably about the end of
October, we had a sudden heavy snowstorm, and the
following night the temperature dropped well
below zero. Early next morning, Father concerned
about the forty or fifty fat young pigs, that had
been feeding out in the stubble, went out to round
them up. Some time later he tramped back through
the deep drifts, with the alarming news that there
was not a pig to be seen anywhere, they had disappeared completely, and he could find no tracks
in the snow. He had covered the whold field
looking for tell-tale lumps under the snow that
would turn out to be little frozen carcasses, but
the snow was even and unbroken. Father was worried
about his deal with Kolb's Restaurant, and we
were anxious about our dear little pigs being
frozen to death.

"Chinook!" shouted Father a few mornings
later, and there across the western sky was that

beautiful arch of soft, clear blue, as the heavy storm clouds were swept towards the east, by the approaching warm wind, that found its way through the Chinook Pass in the Rockies , all the way from the Pacific Ocean. A little while later we could feel the first soft puffs, then came the joyous rushing warm Chinook, pouring over the frozen land, and sending temperatures up in minutes. Soon the snow was melting, and pools and puddles were forming. Men opened their sheepskin coats, and women threw open doors and windows, to let the soft, fresh air in. The blue arch spread across the sky, until the sun broke out of the scattering clouds.

Betty and I saddled Nick and Fatty, and rode out to the wheat field, dreading what we might find, pathetic, huddled little corpses emerging from the disappearing snow. There was a large strawpile in the middle of the field, where the grain had been threshed, and just as we passed it Nick suddenly leaped violently, twisting sideways in mid air and landing, snorting and stamping about,in the still deep drifts. Somehow I managed to stay on his back and struggled to hold him. Betty and Fatty heard the commotion, and a little bit ahead, stopped and turned. Then we saw a marvellous sight, the heavy drift of snow blown up against the strawpile was heaving and breaking.Then there emerged a spotted pig face, round pink snout twitching and sniffing the air. Then another, and another appeared, and out came the whole herd, milling and trampling, and rooting in the snow and straw.

They were soon rounded up, and safely back in their sties. When the snow had gone,we found that the pigs,caught out in the open in the snowstorm, had burrowed a neat round tunnel into the centre of the strawpile,and then had hollowed out a cave large enough for the whole herd. There they had hibernated, warm and comfortable, until instinct told them that the weather had changed, and the snow was melting. They must have been packed in cosily, but how they managed their toilet facilities we never knew, because the straw floor, packed smooth and hard, was clean and fresh.

We played in that lovely cave for the rest of the winter, crawling one by one through the tunnel. The loose straw had been pushed and pressed by the pigs, until the roof and sides of the cave were hard and firm, and the floor fattened. Strangely enough it was perfectly clean and there was no smell, proving animals, even much maligned pigs, can manage their affairs in emergencies, better than most humans.

Our dear Martha, the Yorkshire sow, lived to a good old age, continuing to produce healthy litters of piglets regularly, but she came to a most unfortunate and sad end. The buckets of "slops", all the kitchen refuse of vegetable peelings, left-overs, tealeaves, etc., were taken out to the pigsties, poured into the troughs, and the pigs guzzled it up. Somebody carelessly allow-allowed a cake of Fels-Naptha soap to slip into a bucket of slops one day, and Martha apparently swallowed it. She was found later, unconscious, with soapsuds billowing out of her snout. She did not recover, and Father heaved her heavy body onto a stoneboat, took her out to the pasture and buried her. It was a very sad day for us all.

Feathered Friends

"Four ducks on a pond,
A green bank behind,
A blue sky of spring,
White clouds on a wing;
What a little thing
To remember for years -
To remember with tears!"
William Allingham

There was a remarkable collection of feathered creatures, clucking, quacking and gobbling about Radfords in those days. We had chickens, of course, Orpingtons and White Wyandottes and other varieties. We also had ducks, sparkling white Pekins, that floated serenely about on the pond below the farm buildings. The chickens were housed in a sod house, with a straw roof held up on wire netting, stretched between poles, but they ran loose about the farm, and nested and laid their eggs, in all sorts of unexpected hiding places. From time to time a hen would be missing for a few weeks, and then proudly strut in front of the house with a sprightly train of fluffy little yellow chicks.

There were plenty of eggs, and so we had an original game which we played behind the henhouse where nobody could see us. Eggs were sneaked out of the nests, a couple or so put in our pockets, then two of us would stand about a yard apart. One would throw an egg to the other, back and forth, stepping a foot or so farther apart between each throw, until one of us missed, and the egg smashed on the ground, or broke in our hands, and splattered our faces and clothes, which was very messy. On occasion, one of us when stepping back, would trip and fall, and the eggs in our pockets would be squashed. A pocketful of crushed egg was very nasty, and difficult to explain.

Our flock of large Buff Orpington hens laid

beautiful brown eggs and were prolific in producing new families. So Mother decided that as
they were doing so well, she would try a setting
of turkey eggs under one of the broody hens. She
found a farmer who raised turkeys, and bought a
setting, which the broody hen cheerfully settled
on. Eventually out hatched ten or twelve beautiful, fluffy little turkey chicks. Unfortunately,
young turkeys are very delicate little creatures,
and they die like flies, if exposed to damp or
chill, or even to too much handling or petting.
Mother's little treasures died one after another.
A sad little corpse would be found, crumpled in a
corner of the coop, morning after morning, until
only one was left. This must have been a particularly hardy little fellow, because with Mother's
tender care, and the hen's devoted fussing, he
grew and flourished. He lost his baby down, and
started to grow a few bristly little feathers on
his wings, Father said he would be a fine bird by
Christmas, and so we named him "Christmas", with
never a thought of what Father's remark implied.

One morning we found the mother hen clucking
mournfully about the barnyard with no little
Christmas tagging behind. We hunted everywhere
but could find no trace of him. A large load of
fine sand had been piled behind the house, to be
used for cement to build walls around the cellar,
and to cover the dirt floor. The twins, then
about three, played in the sand with little tin
spades and buckets, making castles and moats, as
we older girls had done on the beaches of Devon
and Somerset in summers past. On this day, when
our little Christmas disappeared, Me Too was
sitting on top of the sandpile, absorbed in her
play, and unconcerned over the lost turkey chick.
We had given up the hunt, when Mother came out of
the house, and called us in for lunch. Me Too
scrambled up from her seat on the sand and there,
in the little hollow where she had been sitting,
squashed flat and very dead, was poor little
Christmas.

I don't remember what we had for Christmas

dinner that year, possibly one of the large Buff Orpingtons, but knowing Father, I rather expect he visited the farmer who raised turkeys, and brought home a good specimen for our festive meal.

Mother became very resourceful, when it came to doctoring ailing animals and birds. I remember one occasion, when she had a sick newborn calf, in a large wooden crate, like a stall, in a corner of the back kitchen. I don't remember what was the matter with it, but Mother fed it with a baby's bottle, and it eventually recovered and was returned to its mother.

A pair of large Emden geese hatched out twelve goslings one spring. The goose had chosen the straw covered roof of the sod chicken house for her nest, flapping up the four or five feet at the back, where the roof sloped toward the ground. Sammy, the gander, was very protective, but did not attempt to get up onto the roof. He stayed close by, gabbling quietly to his spouse, and hissing fiercely at anything that attempted to come too close. Poor Sammy must have had some kind of psychological problem, as he was a compulsive eater. If he could get his beak into a bucket of oats, or wheat, he would stuff himself until his crop was so full, that the grain backed up his long neck until he choked. We would see him, his neck stretched out, eyes closed, staggering about, and somebody would rush to him, hold up his head, and press the grain out of his throat, and down into his crop, until he could breathe again. After a short rest to recover, he would again be hunting for something to eat.

We could watch the nest, with the goose sitting patiently on it, from the back windows of the house, and worried about how she would get the goslings down to the ground when they hatched out. No problem! After a couple of days in the nest the mother goose herded them gently to the lower edge, and they flopped down, one after the other, without coming to any harm. Young goslings are beautiful little creatures, they retain their

greenish, fluffy down much longer than fowl or
turkeys. Their legs and webbed feet, black and
leathery, are large and thick for the goslings'
size, so they look for all the world, as if they
are running about in long, black leather boots.
They grew quickly, and eventually blossomed out
in their handsome beige and white feathers.

The north quarter that year had been seeded
down to wheat and it was doing well. In July the
grain was headed out, and standing thick and
tall.A ripening wheat crop is a beautiful sight.
The heavy heads sway up and down like waves on a
summer sea, the scented breeze ripples across the
silvery green, and as the cloud shadows travel
over the shimmering field, the colour changes
from green to gold to green again.

The gophers had done well that year, too,
raising family after family, and so to protect
the all important wheat, they had to be poisoned.
The strychnine was prepared, the little piles of
poisoned grain were put down beside every gopher
hole around the wheat field. Great care was taken
to keep all animals, horses, cows and pigs, from
getting into the wheat field and the poisoned
grain. The three strand barbed wire fence was
carefully inspected, and the wire gates kept
closed day and night. Unfortunately, nobody
thought about the geese, as they normally stayed
close to the barnyard, and the big slough on the
opposite side of the farmyard. One morning,
Billy, who happened to be our farm help at the
time, came running to the kitchen door, to tell
Mother that the geese were all lying on their
backs in the wheatfield.

Mother and I rushed out, and there they were
lying between the fence and the wheat, in all
kinds of strange positions, stiff and apparently
unconscious, some with their poor leathery legs
sticking straight up. We carried them back to the
barn and Mother sent me up to the house for a
bottle of castor oil and a spoon. Betty, Tommy
and I helped to hold the poor heads up, and
opened the beaks while Mother poured a stiff dose

of the oil down each throat. We stroked the long necks from the head down, to work the oil into their crops. Then we laid them down, now limp and still, on the straw in one of the stalls. We were sure they were dead, and sad tears dribbled down our cheeks. But a miraculous thing happened. A few hours later they were staggering to their feet, flopping about the stall, groggy but definitely alive. They all recovered completely. The castor oil must have been a divine inspiration. Mother couldn't explain afterwards what made her think of dosing the geese with it, but she did say she couldn't think of anything else! Possibly the poison acted so quickly, that the geese had swallowed only a very little before it took effect. The tough crops were not damaged by the poison, and perhaps the oil absorbed it before it penetrated to the more sensitive organs.

Instead of geese, a farmer and his wife, in the English Colony north of Nightingale raised Pekin ducks, and they flourished, producing large families of ducklings. Their farm house was built close to a slough, and in due course, this pond was almost covered with the handsome sparkling white ducks. Roast duck is delicious, and there was a good market for the birds in Calgary restaurants. The eggs made good omelettes, and were used for baking, and the farmer expected to do well with his birds.

At this time, when the crops were ready for threshing, the work was done by outfits that travelled from farm to farm. The farmer's wife had to feed the men. It must have been a gargantuan task for those poor women, unused to the appetites of Canadian farm workers, who expected huge meat meals three times a day - steak with fried eggs on top, plus bacon and heaps of fried potatoes, and mounds of buttered toast for breakfast at 6 A.M.

The ultimate disaster was when a wet spell occurred and the threshing was delayed. The men still had to be fed, and the supplies laid in ahead, soon ran out. Bread had to be set every

night, and baked in the morning, dried apple and
raisin pies, had to be baked by the dozen. Now,
this disaster happpened, during the threshing of
the crop on the duck owner's farm, and instead of
a couple of days at the farm, the gang sat around
in the barn and bunk house for a week, waiting
for the grain to dry out. Short of supplies, and
cash or credit to buy more, the farmer had to
kill off his ducks. The workers ate roast duck,
and dried apple sauce,at least twice a day. There
were very few of those beautiful ducks left on
the pond, by the time the threshing gang eventually pulled away.

Reminiscing about the feathered population at
Radfords during our childhood days, brought to
mind a favourite game that we played one summer.
We had few toys, or traditional games in those
days, and so invented all sorts of pastimes of
our own. Watching the hawks, eagles and elegant
Franklin gulls swooping and soaring effortlessly
on the breezes, against the blue sky, we decided
we should be able to do likewise, if only we had
wings! So, we made paste out of flour and hot
water, and pasted several double sheets of
newspaper together, then pleated the stiffened
paper crosswise, gathered it down the middle so
that it fluted out on each side into "wings".
This was then firmly tied on our shoulders with
bindertwine, and we proceeded to run as fast as
we could down hill, and leap into the air in the
hope that we would glide off into space. Or we
would jump off haystacks or strawpiles, always
with the inevitable result, that we crash landed
with more or less painful effects.

One hot summer day, I had carried a small
cream can of tea, and a paper bag of sandwiches
and scones, to the men who were haying some two
or three miles from the farm, and was returning
across the prairie. My paper wings were fluttering beautifully in the breeze, and I skipped
along imagining myself floating gracefully
through the air.

At this time there was still a good deal of

open range land, to the north east of our boundary, and during the summers a few herds of semi-wild cattle, belonging to the big cattle ranches in the foothills west of us, roamed freely over this area. These animals, turned out to fend for themselves in the spring, would be rounded up in the fall, by the cowboys from the ranches.

On this day , as I was returning from the hayfield, when still a mile or so from the fence along our northern line, I happened to turn around, and to my consternation, saw some twenty or thirty of the range cattle, white faced Herefords, with large spreading horns, pacing silently along, shoulder to shoulder, some fifty yards behind me. As I stared at them,. they stopped and formed a semi-circle, their stolid, white faces staring back at me, completely expressionless. I backed slowly away, then they moved as slowly forward. Then I panicked, turned and ran as hard as I could towards the safety of the barbed wire fenced pasture, my paper wings still flying out from my shoulders. The animals still trotted along behind me, I could hear their hooves on the dry, hard ground, and sure my last day had come, I ran for my life, gasping and panting, stumbling over the rough ground. I stepped into a gopher hole, and rolled over and over. For a moment I lay quite still, then sat up and dared to look back. The animals had stopped, and were standing again in a semi-circle, those nightmare faces staring at me. I was on my feet in a moment, and running again, my wings now hanging in tattered shreds, and I knew the cattle were keeping pace with me. Then, oh heavenly sight! there was the fence. I threw myself on the ground, rolled under the barbed wire and lay gasping for breath, completely winded, with the remains of my wings hanging on the barbed wire. I sat up, and now with the three taut lines of barbed wire strung on the stout cedar fenceposts between us, the big animals did not seem so frightening. They still stared at me with their large brown eyes, but my courage was gradually returning, and I began to realize that they were merely curious and meant me no harm. In another minute I was feeling a little foolish, and rather ashamed of having been so terrified of a few friendly old cows. So I picked myself up, and walked quietly home and told nobody about my fright.

Looking back to that distant day, I can imagine the silent bovine conversation:

"What in Heaven's name is that strange creature with the flapping wings?"

"It's weird! Never saw anything like that before. Is it human?"

"Let's follow it and find out what it is."

"Don't go too close - it looks dangerous!"

"Look out! It's turning around. It might come after us!"

"It must be a bird."

"But it can't fly!"

Frogs

"A frog he would a-wooing go
"Heigh ho!" says Rowley."
Malismata 1611
Thomas Ravenscroft

Spring is slow in coming to the prairies - in the cold, dark days of January and February the sun has little warmth and the deep drifts will be frozen hard and solid. The snow may melt a little in March, and then perhaps a full fledged blizzard will sweep down from the north, and winter returns with bitter cold.

Then it's April, and suddenly spring arrives. The sun glows with a wonderful, kindly warmth, the temperature shoots up, the snow drifts shrink, turning dirty and grey, and soon pools, reflecting the deep blue of the cloudless sky, form on top of the still frozen earth. Gradually the sloughs fill and warm winds from the south and west stir the brown, mossy grass. The birds arrive, horned larks and ducks, prairie chicken scuffle about in the haystacks, hawks soar high above the land, wings almost motionless against the clear sky. And then, a great excitement, a long string of geese in the form of a V sweeps across the sky as they head for their northern nesting grounds, the deep melodious honks an assurance that spring has truly arrived. The gophers awake and crawl sleepily out of their burrows, blinking in the sunshine, and the silvery feathers of the crocus buds appear in pastures. All the world stirs and comes to life with much hustle and bustle.

Then the frog chorus begins. As the long northern twilight fades and the sky darkens, a single croak from the reeds surrounding a slough signals the opening bars of the springtime orchestral performance. Soon the croaks increase until the night is filled with the pulsating thrumming.

We had learned in Natural History class at
school about the strange habit of the bullfrogs
of blowing out huge, almost transparent bubbles
from their throats, like a present day child
blowing bubblegum, while performing their mating
song.I planned to secretly slip out one evening
and go down to a reedy slough in a nearby pasture
to see if I could catch sight of a bull- frog
performing this strange rite.

So one evening after supper I walked across
the road allowance, crawled through the barbed
wire fence and crept quietly towards the slough.
A lemon yellow glow spread across the enormous
dome of the cloudless western sky, with the far
distant jagged outline of the Rocky Mountains jet
black against the fading red streak of the
sunset. But the purple shadow of the night was
already spreading up from the east. It had been
quite warm that day, but now the air was fresh
and cool. As I drew near the slough I went down
on my hands and knees and crawled along through
the reeds until I reached the shallow, muddy edge
of the water. I lay on my stomach and inched
forward, carefully parting the reeds in front of
me. It was almost time for the froggy song to
start, and so I lay quietly peering out onto the
pond which still reflected the clear pale yellow
of the sky. It was very still, no wind and not a
sound to be heard, and then suddenly came the
first croak, so near me I almost jumped, and then
another, and another, coming from different sides
of the slough. Then more and more until the air
was vibrating with the croaking.

I held my breath, and was peering hopefully
through the reeds when without any warning there
came from behind me a great rush of air, and with
a strange whirring sound something tore across
the back of my head, so close that my hair flew
over my face. My arms shot out in front of me, as
I flattened myself face down into the smelly,
liquid mud. I heard a faint splash on the slough
in front of me, and then silence. The croaking of
the frogs had ceased as suddenly as if somebody

had pulled a switch.

After a minute I pulled myself up, the mud running down my face, and wiped the slimy sludge from my eyes. Half a dozen large ducks had zoomed silently low down out of the dark and were now settled a few yards out on the water, swimming slowly away from me, faint spreading ripples catching the last of the sunset glow. In later years I heard that ducks can fly extremely fast, almost as fast as sound, for short distances, and I am sure those ducks were doing their best that night.

I crawled back and then stood up, the mud running down my cotton dress and over and into my leather boots, a horrible, smelly mess. I crept back through the weeds, up the shallow bank and looking back could just make out the ducks, now floating silently in the centre of the pond.

Once again, one loud croak started off the froggy chorus and they were immediately off in full cry again, but I had lost interest and slunk back to the house, where of course I had to explain what had happened to me, and face the laughter and jokes of the family. The galvanized washtub was carried into the kitchen, hot water dipped from the sideboiler, and poured into it. I peeled off my mud soaked clothes and had a comforting hot bath in front of the kitchen range, and then had to rinse my clothes out in the still hot water.

At the time I was humiliated and embarrassed, of course, but it was one of those experiences that have stayed in my memory, and that I would not have missed for anything!

The Wind

"The wind bloweth where it listeth and
thou hearest the sound thereof, but canst
not tell whence it cometh and whither it
goeth."

St. John

Back in those early days the weather, and
particularly the winds, made a greater impact on
the lives of the prairie dwellers than it does in
this enlightened age. Driving to town in an open
cutter, when the temperature might be twenty or
more degrees below zero,with the wind sweeping
over the frozen country, was a grim ordeal. Even
wrapped in buffalo robes, with a large, flat
stone, preheated in the oven, and wrapped in news
papers, under the feet, one could be chilled to
the bone in a short time. Now easier methods of
transportation, insulated houses, sophisticated
heating systems, plus electricity and telephones,
have all helped to make life on the ranches and
farms easier and safer.

The howling winter blizzards, the joyous,
blustering Chinooks, the hot, dry winds of summer
and the whirling duststorms or "dust devils" as
some called them, affected the lives of the
prairie settlers to a great extent. In the spring
of 1910, Father and old Mr. Lane, the carpenter
who had accompanied him from Grandview, to help
him build our new prairie home, were working on
the house.They had just raised the framework of
the four walls of the first storey, when a
violent thunderstorm suddenly swept down from the
north. They had lashed the corner upright beams
together, and Father was at the top of the ladder
when the first furious gust of wind struck. He
felt the heavy frames shake and sway, and hung on
for dear life. Mr. Lane was on the opposite side
and would have been crushed if the walls had
collapsed. Luckily the fierce blast that heralded
the heavy hail and rain lasted only for a few

minutes, and the framework held together.

The winds flowed freely and seemingly endlessly, across the flat or rolling treeless
prairie. In dry years a farmer would see his
precious wheat seed, on which much of the family
livelihood depended, blown out of the dehydrated
soil before it could germinate. In later years,
trees were planted for windbreaks, strip farming
was implemented, and many areas irrigated, all
making the crop prospects more secure. In winter,
when the blizzards swept down from the north, the
range cattle, heads down and tails to the wind,
would drift with the storm over the unfenced
prairie for miles. Many would die of starvation
when the deep snow buried the grass beyond their
reach, and the pathetic frozen carcasses would
come to light in the spring as the snow melted.

Not all the winds brought suffering and
hardship. In midwinter the soft, blue arch across
the western horizon, harbinger of the Chinook,
was a glorious and welcome sight. The marvellous
warm wind that pours down through the mountain
passes all the way from the warm Pacific, and out
across the frozen prairies, may force the temperature up so quickly that it can be twenty below
zero in the early morning, and the snow and ice
be melting by noon. Pools form quickly on top of
the snow and, as children, we would rush out of
the house, shouting with excitement at the sudden
freedom of the outdoors, slosh round in our rubber
boots, make little boats out of pieces of wood,
and sail them on the rippling blue water.

Somewhere on the shingled roof of Radfords
was a slightly loose slat, which this boisterous
westerly wind caused to vibrate, and this made a
steady thrumming noise which could be heard all
over the house. It was only the Chinook that made
it sing that welcome song. Sometimes in the
bitter darkness of a winter's night, we would
hear the first faint murmuring and as the wind
increased, the insistent sound would rise, and
those of us who heard it would snuggle down below

the mounds of blankets, knowing that by sunrise the joyous warm wind would be thawing the frozen land.

There was a story told in those days about the farmer who happened to be in town with his team and sleigh, when the Chinook started to blow. His farm was east of the town, and the Chinook blowing from the west melted the snow so fast that he had to gallop his horses all the way home to keep any snow under the sleigh runners.

On rare occasions, on the open prairies, when the snow falls with no wind to drive it into hard packed drifts, and the temperature is low, the fine flakes fall thickly and gently from the leaden sky, dry and powdery, fine as sand, and the snow lies deep and evenly over the land.

One cold clear moonlit evening, after three days of windless snowfall, I happened to walk out from the horsebarn through the corral into the home pasture. The wind had now risen and was blowing strongly and steadily, the cloudless pewter-coloured sky was spangled with great stars, paled by the silver moonlight. Something strange was happening, I looked down towards my feet, they had disappeared. The even expanse of snow was moving, flowing swiftly and steadily, to the depth of a foot or so, in a solid stream of fine particles, a river of icy white that was sweeping over the land as far as the eye could see. Standing there fascinated, I could hear the faint hissing sound of the fast moving snow, an eerie insistent whispering. This strange phenomenon is called a ground blizzard and only happens when the condition of the snow, force of the wind and the temperature are exactly right.

Another eerie and beautiful sight one still winter's evening, was a display of Northern Lights, the Aurora Borealis. Against the jet black sky the flickering lights, rose, gold, green and ruby red, wavered up and down, sometimes covering the entire perimeter of the sky, from horizon to zenith, creating the impression of our being on the inside of a fantastic flood lit tepee. The colours were reflected on the snow below, shimmering on the white expanse. On this occasion, a particularly cold and still night, we huddled into our coats, scarves, toques and over-shoes and tramped out through the snow to the big pasture, to have a clear view of the sky from horizon to horizon. The world seemed to have flattened to an enormous plane, and as we stood there, marvelling at the enormity and beauty of the display, we could hear a strange unearthly sound, a breathless sort of whispering, a faint crackling, that rose and fell on the still air.

Those Dedicated Men

Bond unknown to me was given,that I
should be, else sinning greatly, a
dedicated spirit.
  Wordsworth, The Prelude.

One cold, grey day in early spring when the
roads were rutted in icy mud, the sloughs brimming, and the last traces of snow disappearing
from the fields, a team of light weight horses,
hitched to the remains of a buggy, stood against
the barbed wire fence about a quarter of a mile
down the road allowance from Radfords. They stood
with their heads down, tangled in their harness,
coated with mud and evidently exhausted.There had
obviously been a runaway, and the driver had
probably been thrown out of his buggy.
    Father and Roy Arnet, in their sheepskin
coats and buckled overshoes sloshed down the road
to the wrecked buggy and with some difficulty un-
tangled the frightened, trembling beasts, then
led them back to the barn. They left the buggy,
which had lost two of its wheels, and seemed to
have been dragged for some distance, leaning
against the fence.
    It was a livery team and buggy, the boney
horses, overdriven, underfed, ill treated, as
they usually were, and naturally apprehensive of
humans, had no doubt been hard to handle. Patches
of raw flesh showed on their legs and sides,
where the leather traces, twisted and tangled,
had flayed their hides.
    The sad beasts were put into stalls, and Roy,
who was fond of animals, soothed them, wiped them
down, fed and watered them, and dabbed the raw
patches with horse liniment. In the meantime,
Father hitched a team to our democrat, and then
he and Roy started off along the muddy road
towards Strathmore to look for the driver.
    The Rector of St. Michael's and All Angel's

Church in Strathmore, at that time, had recently arrived from England to organize and build the new Parish. He was a small, rather frail, middle aged man, with fair hair, and light blue eyes behind gold rimmed pince nez, which was anchored to one ear by a fine chain. Like so many of his parishioners, he had no forewarning of what life on the prairie was at that time. He had lived most of his life in London, and no doubt, had never ridden or driven a horse. But this Parish was his vocation, and he was determined to carry out his sacred duties to his people to the best of his ability. He was always dressed in the correct black clerical garb and white collar, summer and winter, and was strictly orthodox.

Now with a new Parish of hundreds of square miles, that required him to hold services in the scattered communities, he was faced with the alarming prospect of driving himself about with a hired livery team, and buggy or sleigh, depending on the time of the year. He was expected to visit remote homesteads and ranches, hold baptisms, weddings and funerals in farmhouses, and to visit the sick and dying.

On this cold, windy spring day, Father and Roy found him three or four miles along the road allowance leading to Strathmore, sitting on the wet, icy ground and leaning against a fence post, dazed and shaken but otherwise unhurt. He was wet and cold, his heavy black overcoat was covered with mud, and his rubber galoshes had not been sufficient to keep his thin, laced boots from being soaked. Roy found his pince nez, unbroken, hanging on a buckbrush a few yards away. They helped him into the democrat, wrapped a rug around him, and as soon as they reached Radfords, Father mixed him a large, hot toddy, which he drank thankfully. Mother then persuaded him to take off his outer clothes and gave him a blanket to wrap himself in. He sat by the kitchen stove with the oven door open, and his feet in a tub of hot water.

The few Doctors who served the settlers

during the early years were truly dedicated men. They, like the churchmen, had to rely on horses summer and winter to take them to those in need of help, but unable to drive to town. In isolated farm homes they delivered babies, set broken bones, performed emergency operations on kitchen tables and in cases of infectious diseases, had to make arrangements to isolate patients in their homes with the necessary nursing care. The nearest hospital to Radfords was in Calgary, thirty five miles away,where there was also a fever hospital. A doctor's renumeration in those days was often a sack of potatoes, a quarter of beef or a couple of prairie chickens.

The Doctor whose practice was the Strathmore -Nightingale area,had no trouble with his horses. He was Canadian born, and handled his animals well, as he drove or rode over the prairie trails day or night. He had a fine team of strong geldings who could trot tirelessly over the dry prairie in summer,struggle through the snowdrifts in winter, or ford the over-flowing creeks in spring or fall.

Radfords being about half way between Strath-more and Nightingale was a convenient stopover for travellers and the doctor would arrive on a winter's day, in his lightweight sleigh, bundled up in a buffalo fur coat, which in cold weather he could borrow from the Royal Northwest Mounted Police. He would have a short rest,and a strong cup of tea or a quick meal, before going on his way to a patient, or returning to his office to deal with a roomful of ailing people. He told us that sometimes after a sleepless night in a farm home, he would start his team on the homeward trail, tie the reins to the dashboard, then tucked up in his fur rug, would fall into a deep sleep, confident that his horses would jog steadily back to Strathmore.

Our Doctor was a tall, youngish man, slightly stooped, with a bushy dark mustache, and always seemed a little remote, as if he were concent-rating on solutions to his patients' troubles, as no doubt he was. Many were the illnesses that the doctor had to cope with. Besides all the infectious things such as typhoid, diptheria, scarlet fever, there were the inevitable accidents, and such nasty things as ptomaine poisoning and lock-jaw. In the winter there would be pneumonia, frostbite and snow blindness. Blood poisoning was an ever present danger, stepping on a rusty nail, a splinter, or even a scratch, could quickly become infected, and in no time an angry red streak would shoot up a leg or arm. There were home remedies for the less serious troubles. For chest colds, plasters or poultices were made from a mixture of hot mustard and flour, which could blister the skin, if left on for too long. There was goose grease for aching joints and sore muscles. One neighbour who suffered from neuraglia and toothache, told Mother she "otted up a h'onion" and made a poultice with it to hold up against her aching face. A cotton bag filled with salt and heated in the oven was very comforting against a sore back or hip, as the salt held the heat for a long time. The usual treatment for an infection was a handful of boracic acid dissolved in a basin of boiling water in which to soak a hand or foot as the water cooled.

From time to time the Watkins and Rawleigh salesmen in their little horse drawn caravans would call at the homesteads, selling all kinds of remedies, besides many small needs for the farm kitchens, spices, condiments, shoe polish, soaps, and small gadgets. One of the favourite remedies was "eclectic oil" for rubbing on sprains and aches. There would be large jars of hard, dark yellow vaseline which had so many uses, and castor oil, oil of eucalyptus, cascara, and many liniments for humans and animals.

These travelling salesmen would be out on their routes for days at a time, and depended on their customers for a bed at night, and the odd meal, in payment for which they would present the farmwife something special from their wares, a

stoneware pot of jam, a little bag of dried
lavender, or a tin of toffee.

The yellow, top heavy Watkins van with its
high spindly wheels swayed and jolted down the
road allowance on one bright breezy summer
morning. The salesman sat in the front doorway
holding the reins, with his legs dangling down on
the whippletree. He was a small, stocky man with
iron grey hair, cut very short, and his cheeks
were round and rosy like Russet apples. He walked
with a limp, his left leg being a little shorter
than the other, the heel of his left boot was
built up slightly. The big grey horse was plump
and frisky, well groomed, with mane and tail
flowing out in the breeze, the leather harness
was polished, with metal parts gleaming silver in
the sun.

The van drew up to the front of the house and
the salesman tied his horse to a post, then
carried his large flat basket of wares over to
the front door. Mother came out, looked over his
goods and made a selection, then looking closely
at him, asked him his name.

"Babbage, M'm, William Babbage. Just startin'
out on this job." There was a soft burr to his
voice and he drawled his vowels. Mother smiled.

"From the West Country?" She asked. "Somerset
or Devon?"

"Oh, Zumerset, M'm, and O'im goin' 'ome
soon." He chuckled. "Did'n' take too kindly to
prairie farmin'. Worstest mistake Oi ever did
make. Lost all m'money. Took this job to earn a
bit to ta'ake me 'ome and Oi'll be off soon's Oi
'ave enough put aside." He rubbed his hands
together and his small black eyes sparkled at the
prospect.

Mother invited him to have lunch,(dinner as
it was now called) with us, and soon he was
sitting with the family at the oilcloth covered
kitchen table, digging into a large plate of
steak and kidney pudding, with a linen napkin
tucked under his chin. When he had finished and
had wiped up the gravy with a piece of bread he

sat back and sighed happily.

"'Avent 'ad a dinner like that since Oi left Middlezoy!" Mother handed him a slice of dried apple tart and a large cup of tea, some of which he poured into the saucer and supped noisily.

The little man told us that the night before he had stayed with a couple of bachelors on a small farm somewhere north of Nightingale. They had had a stew for supper which had tasted rather peculiar, and after they had finished, one of the men sat back and asked him if he had enjoyed it.

"T'wuz gopher stew, they tole me, and Oi 'ad eaten a 'ole plate of the stuff!" His face turned a little grey. "I was nearly sick right then and there. Them critters be just rats! Rat stew!" He looked slowly round the table at the ring of horrified faces,

To change the subject, Father remarked that he knew the little village of Middlezoy which was not many miles from Yeovil, and had driven his Rover through that lovely countryside. William Babbage then told us he had been a groom since his early boyhood on a large estate near Midddlezoy, but that then his wife died, and a short while later, the titled owner of the manor sold his horses, he decided to emigrate to the Canadian west and try farming. Now he grinned happily, with a faraway look in his eyes, as he talked about his plans to go home and take any job he could find, no matter what, to make a living.

Before he drove on, later in the afternoon, Willie Babbage presented Mother with a little box of crystallized violets, and a large jar of barley sugar, long twisted sticks of golden brown toffee.

The yellow Watkins van did not come our way again for several months, and then it had another salesman. He had no idea what had happened to Willie, but we felt certain he was by then safely back in Middlezoy, happily digging ditches, gardening, washing dishes in the local pub, or hopefully grooming horses again.

In Defence of the Remittance Man

Just as a couple of spoiled apples in a barrelful will taint all the rest, a whole segment of human society may suffer under a permanent stigma, because of the poor showing of a small minority in that group. It seems all the so-called remittance men who emigrated from Britain to the prairies during the colonist era have inherited the stigma of the few "bad apples" among them.

These men were often the younger sons of upper middle class or aristocratic families, who were able to provide them with funds they hoped would start them on careers in a new land. They were usually pblic school educated, some were university graduates, and because of their cultured accents, their unfortunately assured manner,(the British Empire was still in its hey-day) their expensive clothing and obvious background, these young men at first were looked on with suspicion, and understandably, considered snobs. Not all took up homesteading, as eventually some settled into professions or businesses in the towns and cities.

A good majority of these immigrants were responsible young men, who came out with the serious intention of creating a successful future for themselves, and of upholding their family integrity and traditions. The more fortunate came out to relatives or friends who were already settled, and who helped them to make a start. They did not squander their money, they were warned of the pitfalls ahead of them , and while they probably did receive some financial help from their families, they did not become permanently dependent on them. I am sure, because of their education, their integrity, and high standards these men must have had some beneficial impact on the life style of the prairie pioneers of those days.

During the years 1910 to 1914 Father had a succession of these young Englishmen, some from Yeovil, working for him. They came out planning to learn the basics of farming, to experience life on the prairie and they served a sort of apprenticeship at Radfords. They would stay three or six months, and one or two stayed a full year. Then they would sign up for a homestead, or perhaps, decide the hard life was not for them and move on to Calgary or the Coast to an easier future, or return home.

However, the bad apples among them were those young innocents who arrived over confident, cock-a-hoop, full of enthusiasm, it was all a great lark, plenty of money, and they were looked on as fair game by every land dealer, implement agent, and stockman. They were resented, derided, and were the butt of endless jokes. It became a competition as to who could fleece a new arrival of his money the most quickly. They came to Canada inexperienced, naive, over confident and unaware of the hardships they would face. In a short while they would find themselves in difficulties, their money gone, the fun and excitement vanished, and unless their families were able to produce more funds, and certainly not all were financially able to, they were forced to take up any menial job they could find. As Frank Gilbert Roe relates so scathingly in "Getting the Know-How", washing dishes in cafes, sweeping floors, cleaning out the livery stables, etc. Humiliated and disillusioned it was inevitable that many would find comfort in the bottle, if only to bolster their courage. In spite of their outwardly devil-may-care attitude, there were a number of sad, lonely and homesick young men on the prairies in those days, and there were inevitable personal tragedies because of their inexperience.

One young man who had a very sad experience was Gavin. I don't remember his last name. Father told me that he had emigrated from England a year or so before we came, and that his parents had raised enough money to finance him. They were "gentlefolk" but not well-to-do.

Gavin had arrived in Calgary and was making inquiries about homesteading, purchasing land from the C.P.R., and so on, when a man who introduced himself as a land agent, made himself very friendly and eventually persuaded him to buy, sight unseen, a quarter section in the Strathmore district. He showed Gavin a photograph of a house and farm buildings, all neatly fenced, and told him it was a great bargain. The present owner had to sell immediately, it was a tremendous opportunity, and others were waiting to grab it. He assured him he would find some farm machinery in the barn, and would have no trouble acquiring stock and other necessities. The young man, unsuspecting and inexperienced, swallowed the story, paid the man cash in full and received title. With very little of his capital left, he took the train down to Strathmore, located the site, and found the piece of land was bare prairie, unfenced and without a building on it. Also as he found out later, it was unfit for farming, the higher part was too dry and wind-swept for crops, and the rest was mostly alkaline sloughs. Angry and humiliated, he returned to Calgary to find the dealer, but of course he had disappeared. He then went to the police, but apparently there was nothing they could do to help him.

Gavin had not told his parents about this cruel disaster. They continued to send him small remittances from time to time, but he knew they could not afford it, so he assured them he was doing well and needed no more help. He then had to depend on the small wages of a farmhand, barely enough to live on.

One day he rode into Strathmore, put his saddled horse in the livery stable and walked away. It was thought that he might have taken the daily train, which was due about that time, up to Calgary, but he was never heard from again.

Another "remittance man" incident, taken from

my Father"s diary. "That first summer in 1910, due to our many expenses we found our funds running short. I was able to earn over a thousand dollars by putting up seven miles of fencing, cutting 350 acres of wheat for neighbours with our new Massey Harris, and other odd jobs.

On one of my fencing expeditions we camped in a tent eight or ten miles north of Radfords, in very rolling country. The mosquitoes were terrible. A young Englishman, who had been a lieutenant in the British Navy, and who was helping me, was driven temporarily out of his mind. He suddenly threw down his tools and raced away across the prairie. I went for help and later we found him some miles away, wandering about in a dazed state."

These are typical stories of the experiences of the young men who came out on Canada from Britain in the pioneer days. Then came the Great War and the majority of these young men returned to their homeland to enlist, or joined the Canadian Forces. The hey-day of the British Empire was fading, and the day of the remittance man was over.

SOD SHACK

J. KEY

Motor Cars

SOMERSET AND ALBERTA

About the end of the nineteenth century our inventive uncles in Yeovil were experimenting with a "horseless carriage", which turned out to be one of the first motor cars developed in Britain. It worked well, could speed up to about twelve miles an hour, but was expensive to produce and looked on with suspicion by the carriage trade. A few years later the brothers invented an electric car, which also ran well but was considered an expensive foolery, a rich man's toy. However, soon after the turn of the century cars were beginning to appear on the roads about Yeovil, to the immense consternation of the horses drawing phaetons, dogcarts, drays, etc. and their drivers and passengers.As the country roads were narrow and winding, and usually bordered with tall hedges, when it was necessary to pass a horse drawn vehicle the car would have to be driven off to one side, up a bank or into a ditch, the engine turned off and then the snorting, rearing beasts would have to be led past by their indignant drivers.

Father had two cars before we left England in 1910, a small green two seater Rover and a larger red Pannhard, a French production. The Pannhard was a strange car, a convertible on high, spindly wheels and the back seats were on a higher level than the front. One entered the rear seats through a little door in the middle of the back and the seats curved round on each side. Two steps were let down when the door was opened so that the passengers could climb in or out.

We had some wonderful trips into the beautiful country around Yeovil in those exciting vehicles. Mother with a large hat tied down with a voluminous veil, and Father in a long dustcoat. Picnics in the bluebell carpeted larch woods, expeditions to pick primroses along the hedges in springtime or luscious blackberries in the golden

autumn, teas of scones, strawberries and Devonshire cream served in quiet cottage gardens for
mere pennies. On the other hand we seldom went
any distance without having a "blowout" and that
entailed taking off the tyre, patching it on the
side of the road, and then blowing it up again
with a foot pump. Hills were a challenge, and we
all held our breath as the car sputtered, chugged
and roared, and sighed with relief when we reached the top.

And so, in Alberta, when the early Fords
began to appear on the prairie trails Father was
tremendously interested, and before long he
bought a second hand Model T, and drove it home
one bright spring day, sitting "tall in the
saddle" as he bounced and jolted over the gopher
holes and ruts in the trail.

The Ford, with its massive brass trim around
the hood, and the brass rods up each side from
the front of the hood to the top of the windshield, its collapsible top that required a
couple of us on each side, to lower or raise, had
to be cranked by hand. It was very tempermental,
but usually got us to our destination sooner or
later. It was usually driven with the folding top
down, but in bad weather this could be pulled up
and attached to the brass rods that supported the
windshield, and side panels snapped on with press
buttons. These panels had little squares of hazy
celluloid for windows. We had to crank furiously
to start the engine, and the moment it exploded
into action one had to race round and leap up
into the front seat, to adjust the spark and
throttle or it would die.

I remember one occasion when Father was
driving into Drumheller. When negotiating the
long, precipitous, winding road that angled down
the steep hill to the Red Deer river flats, the
brakes suddenly gave out, and we went careening
down, swerving wildly round the hairpin bends on
two wheels and staggering onto the gravel shoul-
ers of the narrow road. Three of us, Betty, Tommy
and I were in the back seat.

Our hair was flying in the wind, as the top was down. We bounced from side to side on the shiny black leather seat, clutching each other, and the sides of the car. Another man was in the front with Father, either one of the farm hands or a neighbour, and when we finally slithered to a halt on the level stretch at the bottom of the hill, he and Father sat perfectly still for a couple of minutes without a word. Then we jounced slowly on to Drumheller, to find a garage and mechanic, who knew enough about this revolutionary new marvel, the motor car, to replace the treacherous brakes.

We had not had the Ford for long before Father decided I should learn to drive it. No driver's licence was required in those days, and although I was only about twelve, I was quite confident and thrilled at the thought of being allowed to drive the car. Father explained the process, let me take the wheel, and being tall for my age I was able to reach the three foot pedals without difficulty.

We started out one day, he and I, and crawled along one of the farm tracks. All went well until we came to a down hill slope, with a wooden gate across the road at the bottom. Father had explained to me how to use the foot brake, and as we started down the little hill and the car gathered speed, Father shouted "Brake! Brake!" but somehow I got my foot on the neutral pedal, and with me frantically clutching the wheel, the car took off, free wheeling down the hill and batttered right through the gate, smashing the slats to pieces. On the other side the road sloped up again, and as the car slowed I was able to find the brake pedal and stop the car. Father said not a word, but got out and examined the front of the car, which was happily none the worse except for a few dents and scratches. I was a bit deflated but Father, believing in "total immersion" made me turn the car around and, after he had cleared the shattered wood from the gateway, drive the car up the hill, then down again. This time I found the brake pedal and we reached the bottom safely.

During the following harvest season, when time was of the essence and a day's delay could result in a field of grain being ruined by freezing rain, or snowed under, an important part of the binder broke down. It was a crucial time, there was a field of cut grain waiting to be stooked, no man could be spared, and so I was sent off by myself in the Model T to Strathmore to get the broken piece repaired.

This was the first time I had driven the car any distance alone. I had no problem on the way into town, but had to wait a long time at the repair shop, and it was already dusk when I finally headed towards home. I had parked the car outside the shop and the mechanic kindly cranked it for me, and got me headed down the one block of main street towards the railway crossing and the homeward trail.

Nowadays eight miles on a paved road with a modern efficient car, even after dark on a deserted, lonely road, would be no problem. That dark night, jolting over the winding, prairie trail, alone in a tempermental Model T Ford, was high adventure.

I chugged slowly along for a couple of miles, when the dark really closed down and I realized I would have to put the lights on. I had a vague idea that there was a button somewhere to press or pull, but I decided I had better stop the car and then fumble around until I found it. To my dismay when I pressed my foot on the brake pedal it wouldn't budge. It took a couple of minutes of semi panic before I remembered the hand brake, then I got the gear into neutral and came to a stop, but I didn't dare turn off the engine in case I would not be able to crank it up again by myself.

I eventually got the lights on and two faint beams shot out along the trail into the darkening night. I crawled down below the driver's seat to try to find what had happened to the foot brake.

A floor board had come loose and jammed under the pedal. I worked away at it and finally got it pushed down into place. Mercifully the engine was still coughing and spluttering. I pulled out the throttle, got it going in low gear, then finally into high gear, and thankfully headed for home.

As the car chugged along the last couple of miles, I could see the faint glimmer of the coal oil lamp, which Mother always put in the dining-room window when somebody was driving home after dark. It was a heart warming welcome sight and I knew that on that night she would be thankful to see me safely home. I reached Radfords without further trouble and the binder was back in the field at daybreak.

Farewell to Prairie Days

In the year 1917 Father's great dream of building a fine new life for his branch of the family began to fade. He had planned, hoped, and worked immensely hard to create a productive farm that would eventually make him secure and established in the New World. Compared to many other colonists of those difficult years he had done exceptionally well, but only to the extent that he had made a living for himself and his family, and had been able to keep out of debt.

He had developed the half section at Strathmore and had bought another piece of land near Drumheller, which had been cultivated and had produced some good crops. A small bungalow and adequate farm buildings had been built on this property.

I am sure Father had planned that his five daughters should marry wealthy ranchers, and probably had hoped that Mother might yet produce a son or two after we were settled at the new Radfords, to carry on the family name, but those dreams never came to pass.

For some time Mother's health had deteriorated and during the summer of 1917 on the advice of our Strathmore doctor she was admitted to Calgary General Hospital for rest and treatment, and so that the doctors there could attempt to diagnose the cause of the bouts of pain and weakness that kept recurring. She came home but did not regain her strength.

The years of hard work and the harsh and primitive way of life on the prairie farm had taken their toll. She was thin and frail, but she never lost her courage or sense of humour. As time went on she grew weaker, and in late December, shortly before Christmas, she was taken back to the Calgary Hospital and after more tests and consultations the doctors decided to operate, but it was too late. She died five days later, on

January 15th, 1918. She was buried in Calgary Cemetery. Father found a little bunch of scented violets in a Calgary florist's shop and placed it in her hands as she lay in her coffin.

Returning to Radfords after the funeral, we realized it was the end of an era, life would never be the same again for any of us. Father was faced with the problem of raising five young daughters by himself, as well as running a household and farm.

Neighbours came to call, bringing their condolences and offering what assistance they were able to give. An English couple, who were farming in the Nightingale Colony a few miles north of us, suggested they move to Radfords, share our home and housekeep for us. The offer was accepted and they and their two little girls came to live with us.

The problem of schooling remained. A young English woman, the widow of a colonist who had died a year or two earlier, had moved to Duncan on Vancouver Island and kept a boarding house. After much correspondence and planning it was arranged that Betty, Tommy and I should go to stay with her and attend the Duncan Public School.

Harry Petter, now forty seven years old, his hair silver white and his hands gnarled and weather beaten with the years of hard work, decided to give up prairie farming and move to British Columbia. He had made the decision to sell the farms, Radfords and the acreage at Drumheller. It was almost two years later, in 1920, that he and the twins joined us at Duncan, and shortly after that Father bought some property at Kye Bay, north of Comox, which he planned to clear and develop into an apple orchard. He rented a comfortable cottage on a cliff overlooking the Strait of Georgia, and the family moved in. Father's sister, our Aunt Lillie, came out from England and took on the onerous task of caring for us. Little did she realize what a boisterous group of girls we were.

Our Father had planned to make a new start in British Columbia; a better life, hopefully something more successful and less strenuous. For myself and my sisters the time was approaching for careers of our own, far from our prairie home, Radfords. From now on that prairie life would be just a memory to store away for years to come.

The depression that followed the Great War now made life difficult for everybody. The payments on the farms that he had sold had ceased and Father had to find work of some kind to keep us. Then his brothers, Ernest and Percy, now prospering with their Westland Aircraft Works and Petter Diesel Engines in Yeovil, offered him the Canadian Agency for Petter Engines. We moved to Vancouver and settled into a new home in the Kitsilano District.

Now our lives changed dramatically. Eventually we found careers for ourselves. Betty became assistant to an eye specialist; Laetitia having finished public school went on to Normal College, and with her degree in Education went up to Fort St. John and taught in the public school there. Madge joined the staff at Painters Lodge, then a flourishing summer resort hotel in Campbell River, and eventually married the brother of the owner of that Hotel. Barbara joined the staff of the Bank of Montreal in Vancouver, and I worked for the Canadian Bank of Commerce, in Vancouver and was then transferred to Red Deer, Alberta. Predictably we both married Bank men.

In 1925 Father married Ethel Vulliamy and when he retired from the Petter Engines Agency on a small pension they moved to Duncan and built a comfortable bungalow where they lived happily until he died in 1943.

Books may be ordered by mail from :-

Martel Publications,

101 - 141 Bushby St.,

Victoria B.C. V8S 1B3

(604)-384-8338

Price $10.50   plus $1.00   postage   and
handling.